COMMONSENSE

COMMONSENSE SCHOOLING

Based on the indications of Rudolf Steiner

ROY WILKINSON

The Robinswood Press

Stourbridge   England

Commonsense Schooling

First Published 1975
© Roy Wilkinson 1975
Reprinted 1978 and 1982
This edition 1990

ISBN 1 869981 08 1

This edition is published jointly by the author and
The Robinswood Press

Printed by Billing and Son, Worcester.

Contents

Preface

Rudolf Steiner was born in 1861 and died in 1925. His literary and lecturing output was prodigious. In Europe and in most parts of the civilised world there are groups of people well acquainted with his work, yet it is a surprising and recurring phenomenon to meet so many people, even the learned, to whom the name is known but to whom it means little or nothing.

In this connection the words of a well-known American, Russell Wheeler Davenport, may be of interest. Russell Davenport was at one time a writer in the periodical 'Time', managing editor of 'Fortune', and then chief editorial writer of that glossy and influential magazine 'Life'. He died in 1954 and at the time he was working on a book, since published under the title 'The Dignity of Man'. In this book he speaks of Rudolf Steiner: . . . 'That the academic world has managed to dismiss Steiner's works as inconsequential and irrelevant is one of the intellectual wonders of the twentieth century. Anyone who is willing to study those vast works with an open mind will find himself faced with one of the greatest thinkers of all time, whose grasp of the modern sciences is equalled only by his profound learning in the ancient ones.'

Rudolf Steiner wrote 20 books; his collected essays are published in 9 volumes. He gave over 6,000 lectures. At present a complete edition of his works is being prepared and will contain (in German) 350 volumes. His books and lectures cover most fields of human endeavour. In his day he was the recognised expert on Goethe. He wrote or lectured on philosophy, psychology, christology, evolution, sociology, history, medicine, agriculture, dramatic art, education. He himself created the new art of movement, eurhythmy, and he was a practical artist in sculpture and architecture.

Rudolf Steiner's genius was such that he could meet experts on their own ground, whether they were farmers, doctors or theologians and he could suggest new lines of thought in all fields.

These are impressive and remarkable facts, perhaps even bordering on the incredible, but, in a sense, they are also externalities. Rudolf Steiner represents something much more fundamental than erudition.

The world, the cosmos, and the human being are mysteries which each generation seeks to understand in its own way. Our present age stands under the shadow of natural science and science has a habit of giving explanations from a materialistic point of view. But ideas on matter are changing. Matter itself does not seem so solid and reliable as it did a hundred years ago and it is admitted that its essence remains yet to be discovered. Planetary spheres are being explored and all sorts of information gathered, but let us remember that the instruments concerned can only record those things to which they are attuned. There may be other influences, ...not recorded. With regard to the human being, scientists and philosophers now speak of different spheres of consciousness. Three stages are known to us: waking, sleeping and dreaming. There may well be others and then the world of matter, as of cosmic space and the human being, may appear differently.

Years ago, the philosopher, Kant, put forward the idea of the boundaries of knowledge. This has been superseded and now we recognise that the boundary of knowledge is our own capacity and that if capacity is developed, the boundary is pushed further back. We all accept the existence of a physical world. Most of us accept the existence of a spiritual world or a Kingdom of God. With our ordinary senses we are aware of the physical world. Could it be that other senses can be develc ͻed whereby we are aware of the spiritual world?

Goethe asserted that this was the case. With our everyday senses we perceive the physical world but to perceive the spiritual world we need other organs of perception. This is the fundamental point that has to be made clear in speaking of Rudolf Steiner. Throughout history there have been personalities who possessed higher faculties, as, for instance, the prophets of the Old Testament and the temple initiates. In our own times, Rudolf Steiner was one, who, in high degree, possessed higher powers of cognition. When such a statement is made, the usual reaction of the mind, particularly in the English speaking world, is to think of something vague, dreamy or mystical. Again let Russell Davenport be quoted: 'Steiner was no more of a mystic than Albert Einstein, — he was a scientist rather, but a scientist who dared to enter into the mysteries of life.

To make things a little clearer let us think of all the experts that exist in their own particular fields. Each one has some experience and knowledge over and above that of his neighbour. The one may be initiated (and the expression should be noted) in the world of finance; another in law. So in a certain sense each one could be termed an 'Initiate'. These, however, are still earthly matters. Rudolf Steiner was able to perceive worlds other than those which can be described by the physical senses. But mere perception is only a beginning. With physical eyes we see a physical world, but seeing is not necessarily understanding.

To understand, another faculty is required, namely, thinking. With spiritual eyes, the spiritual world is visible, but here also seeing is not understanding. A faculty similar to thinking, in order to be able to dissect, analyse and correlate, is necessary.

The power to penetrate beyond the physical can be developed out of the modern western way of thinking. We are not concerned here with Yoga or any out-dated system of oriental mysticism, and it was this power that Dr. Steiner possessed. Thus we can speak of him as the modern initiate. Steiner, with his vision and capacities, was able to penetrate into the spiritual world. He was able to read the records imprinted there, to comprehend and describe the spiritual background of earthly events, — and he does this as a scientist. He also shows how others can follow the path.

If we accept the possibility of attaining a knowledge of supersensible worlds or of developing an extended consciousness, the question may arise as to purpose. Where does it lead? Let another famous American, Abraham Lincoln, answer this: 'If we would know more where we come from and whither we are going, we would know better what to do and how to do it'.

The search for wider knowledge is an eternal quest. Wider knowledge has practical applications. Thus we see Steiner's indications bearing fruit in practical spheres. One of these is agriculture, with suggestions for rejuvenation of the soil, overcoming disease and promoting healthy livestock. Another is medicine, with indications of a new approach to illness and new remedies, including one for cancer. A third is education, with schools and schooling based on a comprehensive understanding of the human being.

Wider knowledge gives the key to the understanding of history and evolution. With Steiner's explanations we understand how man, in the course of history, has lost an original power of spiritual perception. He has exchanged it for a material outlook on the world and abstract thinking; but coupled with this is his own development as an ego-conscious individuality. This gives a pointer to the future, for, from now on, man can awaken new powers within himself in freedom.

Wider knowledge helps to an understanding of ourselves and the world. If we can learn more of our origin and destiny we know more about our own life and what to do with it. We think of an existence after death. Perhaps we could think of an existence before birth. We might in this connection consider the inequalities of life and the varying capacities of people. Perhaps we as individualities are responsible for what we are and what we have. Our birth may well be 'a sleep and a forgetting' but we come into earth existence nevertheless with gifts, potentialities, desires and aims. In this event we no longer consider ourselves as being thrust blindly or accidentally into life but are indeed masters of our own fate.

Commonsense Schooling does not deal with the spiritual background from which Rudolf Steiner derived his inspiration but concerns itself only with the practical application of his ideas in education.

Roy Wilkinson, Forest Row, Sussex
January 1978

Foreword to the 1990 edition

Commonsense Schooling was first published in 1975. Since then many changes and developments have taken place in the world at large and many innovations have been advocated in the field of education, particularly in the most recent times. However, new ideas (for example, for testing, the core curriculum, extra pay for specialists and so on being implemented in schools in Britain) often do not touch the root of the malaise and in no way invalidate the main thrust of this book. In fact they strengthen it. Education is not a matter of an efficient production line but is concerned with human development.

One or two matters, however, may have less relevance today than when originally mentioned: inflation has its ups and downs; transcendental meditation may be now considered old-fashioned; instead of machine, one might say computer. None of these items was felt to be of sufficient importance to warrant a costly revision to the text. It therefore appears in this new edition as in the original.

Roy Wilkinson, Forest Row, Sussex
Spring 1990

1

Education Today

This book is addressed to all those who are dissatisfied with present-day education — dissatisfied not only on account of shortages and deficiencies in the external sense, but also because they feel that modern education does not provide the necessary spiritual nourishment and support for the whole being of the child.

It is easy to talk of an age of transition. Evolution means a continual state of transition, yet vaster changes have probably taken place in way of life and in mental outlook during the last hundred years than in any other epoch. We are experiencing enormous and apparently endless progress in technology as the machine takes over and dominates human life. Technology has become the new god and in his service we sacrifice irreplaceable natural resources and tolerate universal pollution.

An advanced technology means that intelligence is, so to speak, built into the machine so that the person using it needs to think less and less. To make matters worse, the human being today, at least in our western civilisations, is being continuously bombarded by sense impressions. He has little opportunity to come to 'himself'. Insidiously, the externalities of life sap his strength. That is perhaps why there is such a growing interest in such things as transcendental meditation. Man's struggle today is to preserve his identity as a free spiritual human being.

We might also ask what acceptable philosophy of life present civilisation, which includes the school, has to offer. The widely accepted picture is of a world having accidentally evolved from some primeval mist and heading towards a state of ultimate frigidity. Man is an accidental product of a series of developments out of primeval mud. The struggle for existence is the process of evolution. Explanation of the world and man is given from a physical-chemical-technical point of view. So what purpose is there in life? What is the sense of existence?

By contrast, the church, or religious instruction where it exists, tells of a God-created world. No bridge is made between this and the scientific explanation and an unresolved conflict is produced in the soul.

Crime mounts, racial confrontations increase, industrial troubles grow and we see the social order on the point of disintegrating. With rampant inflation and unemployment it is scarcely necessary to mention the chaos in the economic field. The traditional source of spiritual impulse — religion — has almost dried up.

This is the world into which our children are born and this is the world in which they grow up. For our own sakes as well as theirs, some of us would like to change it, but a feeling of helplessness afflicts the individual when he considers the overwhelming odds.

We have programmes and experiments galore, good intentions and goodwill, yet national and world conditions deteriorate. Society is created by human beings. An improved society postulates an improvement in standards of behaviour. Regeneration of society can only start with the individual. If there is to be a moral order and a just social order, it must be brought about by human beings who *will* it, or possibly by those to whom these things have become second nature. This is where education and the school are immediately concerned.

We have, of course, to recognise that the school is a reflection of society. We have to admit that parents fail. In some cases parents have wholly abrogated their responsibilities; in others, environmental pressures are too strong. It would seem, however, that society as a whole is less likely to reform and alter the school system than that enlightened teachers, supported by enlightened parents, grasp new ideas and put them into practice. This would at least be a leaven. It is not being suggested that all our social evils are due to our educational system, but it might be fair comment to say that there would be fewer if education were more inspiring.

Children need to learn skills, to gain knowledge, to develop a social awareness and to generate an active mind and will. In present circumstances, however, and in the future, education must do more than these things. It must seek to establish an inner strength and moral fibre to withstand the attacks on the individuality. It must also become curative, seeking to create a harmony in the being of man.

Furthermore, although it is one of the tasks of education to disseminate knowledge, we must bear in mind that the sum total of knowledge mounts, not in arithmetical, but in geometrical progression. It would seem therefore that education must, among other things, concern itself less with actual learning than with developing a flexibility and adaptability of mind in order to cope with situations, the nature of which cannot be foreseen.

Do we provide this sort of education? Do our schools meet the demands of the times? Do they meet the needs of the children?

Education has become mainly training and instruction. It is almost like a cropping plan imposed on a garden with little regard to soil or climate. Perhaps a better comparison would be with the production line, which may be satisfactory for producing inanimate objects, but less so in dealing with human beings. In recent years things have admittedly become far less formal and rigid as far as the primary school is concerned, though a certain 'processing' often takes place in later stages. Some primary schools now work the 'integrated' day. This means that there are no timetables and no set lessons. The children arrange themselves in groups and each group follows some particular interest for a while with the teacher supervising and helping where necessary. After a time the groups switch round. It is learning through discovery and it is hoped that the children will pick up the essentials on their own initiative. Objections can be raised to the arrangement but it is certainly a vast improvement on the rigid way of teaching of fifty years ago.

Then, in the secondary school, specialists take over. For the pupils, passing an examination is the desired goal. If the modern primary school has a relatively harmonious atmosphere, the secondary school has a disjointed one. The time-table is arranged to get in the requisite number of periods for each subject, irrespective of what subject precedes or follows. For each subject there is a different teacher and often a change of room is involved. There is no organic sequence of instruction, no rhythm in the day. Periods are short and children just get settled down to one lesson when it is time to change. Time is invariably lost in changing classrooms. The child's school day is an endless succession of disjointed events and personalities in those formative years when it might have been thought that continuity and order are essentials. Have we any right to complain that children lack concentration?

This is not to say that there is no place for specialists and the case is different for children after the age of fourteen, as will be explained later.

There is continual controversy in the matter of religious instruction. Strangely enough, considering the general apathy towards it, religion is the only compulsory subject in the syllabus in England. Perhaps its importance is still imprinted in the ancestral memory. I have witnessed the most strange things put over in the morning assembly, which is supposedly an act of worship. If substance is not brought into these matters, they simply induce ridicule. The government may decree that religion shall be taught but unless it lives in the hearts of the teachers, children will reject it.

The whole question of staff relationships and salary structure is also something which might be re-examined. It might well be concluded that ideas adopted from big business have no place in the school.

Many educationists, parents and social workers are aware of the problems, yet no specific way of dealing with them has so far been built into an educational system. The fact that all is not well in education is obvious from the amount of thought and effort being given to improve it. The whole of the present organisation, subjects taught and teaching methods are continually being subjected to scrutiny and reappraisal. Endless proposals, experiments and investigations are made. Such activity is to be welcomed, for where there is movement there is life.

With the idea of giving children equal opportunities and breaking down class barriers, comprehensive schools have been introduced. We can here recognise positive, social impulses at work. Unfortunately, things do not always turn out as planned.

Good and necessary though change is, it is essential to consider it on its merits. It cannot be said that every innovation is for the best and the fact that education deals with human beings should never be overlooked.

Experiments are carried out, for instance, to investigate the processes of learning, with the aim of getting the child to learn more quickly or to do advanced things earlier. The trend is to treat the human being as something which can be manipulated. This is undignified, to say the least, and the more fundamental question must be asked as to whether the speeding up of learning is a good thing anyway.

One of the latest ideas in the educational field is programmed learning. The child learns one fact, then comes the next. Each fact is 'reinforced'. The idea is new, and lends itself to mechanical contraptions. Some teachers take it up with enthusiasm and, as it is a novelty, so do some pupils. However, in such an arrangement, are we really thinking of learning for educational benefit? When a child has learnt something, it needs time to reflect on it, to digest it, to bring it into relationship with everything else that it knows. A machine can instil a string of dates quickly into a child's mind. It can, no doubt, do the same with facts and figures about the universe, but whether it can awaken a feeling of awe and reverence for the universe, as can a teacher who has experienced such feelings, is a different question. Any teacher talking to a group of youngsters knows the endless questions that can arise from some piece of information imparted. The child's imagination and activity are stimulated. But a programme must be followed and it immediately clamps down on the awakened interest. As a means of instilling facts, the programme may be efficient. As an educator, it is a monster.

Similar arguments apply to the use of radio and television. If something is available which fits in with what one is teaching, it may be a useful supplement. The mass media, however, can never enter into the subtleties which play between pupil and teacher in the personal relationship. It is each teacher's task to meet the needs of his particular pupils, not to make them adapt themselves to some outside scheme. The impersonal corporation can probably produce or reproduce something with greater accuracy and perfection, but it cannot gauge the child's need or react to the child's reaction.

The wind of change is blowing through all sections of our society. What will be the shape of education in and for the future?

There can be no final answer. The human being evolves; social attitudes change; the community develops. Education and methods of education will evolve too. What is right in one place and at one time will be wrong in another. The one thing that remains constant, although his capacities and needs change, is the human being.

Man is not an animal to be trained. He is not an inanimate object to be processed. He is a being of body, soul and spirit. Through his physical body he is related to the world of matter. He has a life force in common with the plants. Emotions and sensations he shares with the animals. In his inner core he is an individual possessed of the divine spark. Man is related to all things and is the centre of all things. His evolution is not yet complete. He has the possibility of infinite development.

Teachers, parents, the community at large must take a fresh look at man. In particular they must consider the nature of the child and what they expect from education. The starting point for any discussion must be centred in man, and any deliberation or experiment that begins elsewhere misses the point. This book is a practical attempt to define these matters as they appear in our present age, and to draw the appropriate conclusions.

2

Purpose of Education

Why educate? Primitive man seems to have got along without formal education. The other species of mammalia do not seem to need it. In a relatively short time after birth most animals are sufficiently mature to fend for themselves but the human being requires years of growth and development. This vital difference between man and animal may give us a clue to the purpose of education.

The animal is conditioned by nature. Its surroundings and even its self-created environment are a part of its nature. The bird's nest is not a home such as humans have. Man elevates himself above nature, forms it to another use and transforms it. He invents. The animal works instinctively; the human being has faculties which are on a higher level than instinct. He thinks. Animal and man have feelings and emotions, but only man becomes a self-conscious individual, endowed with the human spirit.

The animal very quickly comes into possession of its adult faculties. The human being requires a slow introduction to the world and needs time to develop his capacities and to take full possession of his body. The nearer human beings are to the life of nature, the less education they need. The more complex civilisation becomes, the greater the necessity for an introduction to it, and the greater the necessity for man to strengthen his inner being to cope with the difficulties and distractions which civilisation brings.

The human being is a complicated creature. In spite of a certain uniformity, one cannot say what his reaction to any particular stimulus will be. One can establish certain similarities and patterns, but the genius *homo sapiens* is not only complex, but each member of it is equally so. For this reason it is difficult to formulate any hard and fast rules about education.

The Butler Act of 1944 laid down that children should be educated according to age, ability and aptitude. The intention was wholly positive. It was to provide for the gifted, the non-gifted, the slow learners, the backward and the maladjusted and perhaps the ruling is as good as can be formulated in a general sense.

The interpretation of that ruling, however, can be as wide as the variations in human opinion. One American writer advocates teaching a child to read at 14 months. That child is then being taught according to age, ability and aptitude, but is this educationally beneficial? A monkey can be taught tricks according to ability and aptitude; so can, a child. In fact, a child may have all sorts of abilities and aptitudes, some perhaps immoral or antisocial; should these, too, be encouraged?

Some time ago it was fashionable in certain circles to test a child's aptitude in order to decide on a career. Thus tests might show an aptitude for medicine, and so the stage would be set for the child to become a doctor. Then it was discovered that, human nature being what it is, a person has likes and dislikes, and the child did not want to become a doctor but an engineer. So ideas shifted and it was thought that a third-rate but interested engineer would be more appropriate to the personality than a first-rate, bored doctor. Who shall deny that, if the interest is there, the child might also ultimately become a *first-rate* engineer?

The Bulter Act ruling on ability and aptitude, therefore, unless modified by many other points of view, can have strange results. It can mean that if a child has no aptitude for languages, he should not learn them; no understanding for science, he should drop it; no ability for handwork, he should leave it alone. Education may thus become very onesided, unaware that an ability or aptitude can be dormant, that it is important perhaps to cultivate a faculty which is not immediately apparent, and that all-round experience can only be given by an all-round education. Whether the child fully understands or has the ability and aptitude is not, in the first place, of prime importance. A certain subject can give a certain experience even if it is not fully understood and children should not be denied the experience.

If we were to ask any group of people for their views on the aims of education, the replies would very likely be as varied and numerous as the individuals concerned: to learn something, to build character, to prepare for life, to learn how to learn, to develop talents, to learn responsibility, to harmonise the faculties, to learn to become a good citizen. Undoubtedly all these statements are worthy and correct, but a little vague.

Various groups have emerged with definite ideas on education. One maintains that the giving of knowledge is all-important. The 'progressives' consider that the child should develop seemingly untrammelled by adult interference. A third group thinks that education should be steered towards some definite religious point of view.

Whatever ideas may be expressed, education is a mixture of cultural and vocational aims. The original meaning of 'to educate' was 'to nourish', and this is the cultural side; but it must also give some of the practical skills for vocational purposes. Education is something which takes place between two poles. On the one hand is the child and on the other the world into which it is born. The agents between are the parents and teachers, with their knowledge, gifts, capacities, experience, temperaments and, alas, their limitations.

Although we may think of education as something belonging to the early years, it is really something which continues throughout life. It is the early education, however, which conditions the later. 'The child is father of the man'; whatever is experienced in childhood has its effect throughout the whole of life. Thus, the long-term effects of early education must be seriously considered. There are powers which develop late in life and the child has to be educated so that he can use them when they become available. As the physical body needs nourishment, so does the mind, and it is the task of education to provide it.

Today education has become mainly informative, but it would appear that another role, already mentioned in the first chapter, must be allotted to it: it must be curative. In the midst of the present forces of destruction some counterweight must be provided to achieve balance and help restore an integrated personality.

As teachers and parents we have to ask ourselves what sort of world outlook do we want our children to have, and how are they to be occupied? This is particularly relevant in view of the greater leisure time anticipated. It is not easy to answer these questions and if suggestions are put forward here, they must not be looked upon as watertight or as excluding everything else. The whole field of human development and education is too vast to be absorbed at one viewing, so that a breakdown into sections is essential.

The society we live in, whatever it may be, will make certain demands on us. The Red Indians had to learn to track and shoot with the bow and arrow; the Australian Aborigines to find their water holes; the present Tonga islander must cultivate his quota of banana trees. To live in our society there are other elementary requirements.

Although some people manage to get along without it, most of us would be in difficulties without an elementary knowledge of reading. The same applies to writing and to arithmetic. There are also certain practical accomplishments which are useful, if not absolutely essential — such things, for instance, as the ability to mend a fuse, use a hammer and saw, cook an egg, even drive a car. Further than this, a sharpening of wits is essential, if not exactly to defeat the law, at least to understand it in relation to such matters as income tax returns and official documents. Correct observation, initiative, memory, self-confidence, powers of thinking and judgement are no lesser necessary abilities than are the capacities of reading and writing.

We are concerned here with something that is perhaps better described as training rather than education, although, of course, all things are educative in some way. In a general way, then, it can be said that one of the tasks of education is *training in intellectual and manipulative skills.*

In so far as a child is born into a community which has a certain way of life, he has to conform. He has to adapt himself to his environment and to be made familiar with it. He is born at a certain time, in a certain place, to certain parents, within a certain race or nation, but he is today also a world citizen. He needs, therefore, orientation as to the nature of his society and of the world.

Society has rules and conventions. A person living alone in a field with no neighbours within sight or earshot may go about naked, play the trumpet all day and do pretty well what he likes; but as soon as there is a community, the rights of others must be respected. It is not necessary to argue that lying and stealing are antisocial. A sense of responsibility is necessary, a sense of what is right or wrong. Into this category then comes moral education. In a general way, then, it can be said that a further aim of education is *an awakening of social conscience.*

Every person has some sort of creative urge within him. Some, the fortunate ones, can bring it to expression in their work, but often only insufficiently. Everyone has some need of self-expression. One person finds it in gardening, another in painting. No one is happy without some outlet for creative activity. Every personality is different and wants to follow his own interest or develop his own talents. This is perhaps of great importance today to balance the stresses of modern civilisation. Education has, therefore, to reckon with this factor and provide the necessary knowledge, information and introductions. A third aim of education is thus *cultivation of means of self-expression.*

There is yet a fourth aim which is much more difficult to define. It has to do with that distinctive feature of the human being, in contrast with the animal, which we term the human spirit. It has to do with our outlook on life. In England we are a Christian community with some belief in the divine and in the eternal verities. We may not know what the end result will be but the Christian path is one of individual improvement. This fourth factor is then something like a betterment of human nature. The school takes an individual so far along the path of life, and then hands him over, as it were, to himself. The self, however, must be strong enough to cope and in this sense of striving towards perfection, development becomes self-development. We are seeking for some definition which will include the development of individual forces, capacities, understanding, initiative — all these things which are particularly connected with the human spirit. In individual development one becomes conscious of what 'I am and no-one else is, of what I know and no-one else knows, of what I can do, and no-one else can do.'

Pestalozzi comes near what we mean when he says: 'The higher object of education is to develop the human being so that he can make free and independent use of all the faculties which the Creator has implanted within him, and to direct all these faculties to the perfection of all human existence, so that every human being, in his own particular situation, can act as an instrument of that almighty and all-wise Power which called him into being.

'It should be realised that the aim of instruction is nothing more and cannot be anything more than the furtherance of humanity through the harmonious development of the forces and capacities in human nature.'

Rudolf Steiner expresses the ideal in these words: 'Our highest endeavour must be to develop free human beings who are able of themselves to impart purpose and direction to their lives.'

This ideal, this ability to find and develop oneself, can be called *spiritual development*.

We now have four headings under which we can consider the purpose of education. They overlap and interweave. Other expressions, possibly equally good, could be found. However, they are sufficiently comprehensive to contain the generalisations often made, and are also more concrete:

(1) Training in intellectual and manipulative skills;
(2) An awakening of social conscience;
(3) Cultivation of means of self-expression;
(4) Spiritual development.

Immediately, however, comes a difficulty — some of these aims appear to contradict each other. Can we, for instance, train in skills without imposing on the personality? Does what is necessary for community life agree with the requirements for individual development? Does one have the right to colour a child's outlook?

As mentioned in Chapter 1, traditional education has basically concerned itself with the first aim — the imparting of information. It is true that there have been divinity lessons; also moral injunctions and exhortations, but these have not been consciously and consistently incorporated in the curriculum or methods of subject presentation.

The pendulum has swung to the other side, in fact, in the free-for-all, do-as-you-like type of school where training and learning go by the board and the emphasis is on the unfolding of the personality and spiritual development, if it can be called this in such a context. The advocates of these schools have overlooked the fact that self-determination, the ability to give oneself direction, is nonexistent in a child and is meaningless until maturity. The classical example of this is the child at one of these schools crying his heart out. A visitor approached and asked what was the matter, since this was a place where a child could do as he wished. In answer the boy sobbed, 'Nobody will tell me what I ought to like to do.'

It is important that a child should acquire skills. It is important that he should become a responsible citizen. It is important that his faculties should have free play, and that he should take steps himself along the path of evolution, consciously.

So we must put the question: what is the style, structure, curriculum of an education which seeks to do justice to the whole of man, which teaches him the skills without destroying his initiative, which allows self-expression without impinging on the rights of the community, and which will eventually set him in the world as a free moral individual able himself to give purpose and direction to his life?

All learning contributes in some way. It is difficult to separate subjects and say, 'This is a skill.' Writing and reading are certainly skills but have a social impact — in learning them other qualities are also gained. Thus it is not a matter of teaching one particular subject to fulfil one particular aim, but of teaching all subjects with all the four aims listed above in mind. The teacher must say to himself, 'I am teaching a skill. How can I use this to further social responsibility, to free creative powers, to develop the human spirit?' In geography, for example, making a map is a practical skill, but the knowledge so gained can lead to a better understanding of the world and its peoples.

We shall have to discuss subjects and their method of presentation in this light, but before doing so, let us look at the 'material' with which we are working, i.e. the human being in his early years.

3

The Nature of the Child

In H.G. Wells' story *The History of Mr. Polly*, there is a superb description of the father and the mother doting on their baby, the most desirable and adorable thing in the world, marvelling at the delicacy of his hair, going into transports of delight at his gurgling sounds, smothering him with affection, and rapturously kissing his small toes. In the course of time the same baby becomes 'that dratted boy'.

It is an experience that more or less all parents undergo. From a tiny creature of purity, innocence and delight there emerges the awkward, gawky, ungainly and often cheeky youth of 14 and the precocious adolescent of 16 or 17. Fortunately, the process seems self-correcting. Generally a reasonable, self-possessed young man or woman emerges in the twenties, an energetic and capable person in the thirties and forties and, we hope, a gradually maturing personality as yet more years go by.

The process is one of growth, physical and mental. We notice growth in children because it is then more obvious. We have already noted how the animal matures quickly after birth and is relatively soon able to fend for itself. The child develops slowly. Nature has ordained something different for the human being than just catering for his bodily needs, and has organised a long and a gentle growth. The child takes time to 'wake up', that is, to come to adult consciousness. As grown-ups we do not like it if we are rudely awakened. We can well imagine that the same thing applies to a child in the matter of 'growing up'. We said already that the tendency of modern education is to get the child to do adult things earlier. By so doing, education is working contrary to human nature.

Experiments and observation may decide that children are capable of this or that, or have an interest in some particular field, or that some method of presentation appeals to them. From such research have developed the tricks and expedients which may help a child to learn but do not necessarily educate him. The conclusions drawn from it, moreover, may be incorrect. Interests may be artificially induced. One must remember that the small child is very imitative. If father is tinkering with the car and the boy picks up a spanner and does likewise, it is not to be interpreted that here is a budding engineer or even that he has an interest in things mechanical. He is very properly and simply doing the same as his father. If the child is in the garden and pulls up the carrots while the parents are weeding, there is no blame attached to the child. He is not a malicious destroyer of good food and effort. It is neither wickedness nor a manifestation of a particular interest or non-interest in gardening. The child is simply following the dictates of his nature which says, 'Do as the people around you do.' Children are curious and interested in everything and human nature urges them to try things.

One might pose the question as to what is the right age for children to learn to read. Some say as early as possible, even as early as 14 months. Others say as soon as the child shows aptitude. However, the small child picks up a book or a paper and 'reads' long before he has the faculty, simply because all the people around him are doing this. It might just as well be argued that a child should eat as many sweets as he likes because he has developed a liking for them.

While, therefore, experimental psychology may teach us a great deal about processes and manifestations and lead to improvements in training, it does not give the clue to education in the real sense. For this a study needs to be made of child development which not only observes the reactions to stimuli, etc., but also tries to catch the undertones of the child's true nature.

We mentioned the process of growth. The clue to the understanding of human life is that it is something which develops in time. The child is not a small edition of the adult but a potential adult. He is in a state of 'becoming', but in both physical and mental constitution he is different from an adult.

Even perfunctory comparison of child and adult will show this. The head of the child is relatively large, the limbs are unformed. Watch a young child run — it seems as if the head is floating along and the limbs are tottering after it. Compare this with the rhythmic striding of an adult where the limbs carry the head. The rhythmic system of the small child is also undeveloped; his breathing is irregular compared with an adult's, his pulse beat is faster, and his temperature can rise and fall very quickly.

The mental processes are also quite different. If we, as adults, have a problem requiring logical thought, we can sit down — or walk about, which sometimes makes the thought processes function more easily — and put our minds to it. If we find that for some reason our sympathies or antipathies are running away with us, we can cry halt. If we decide that there is some job which has to be done, however unpleasant, we can tell ourselves to do it. Our faculties of thinking, feeling and willing can, to some extent, be guided by whatever it is in us that exerts this power. The child, on the other hand, is much more at the mercy of his natural forces. The primeval power gushes through his will and feeling without recourse to reason. In fact, the adult way of reasoning is virtually absent in the child up to about the age of twelve. Anyone who has witnessed inexperienced parents *arguing* with a baby will know what is meant. The child, says, 'I don't want it', and reasons why it should have it are of no avail whatsoever.

On the emotional, imaginative plane the child is much

Among the impressions that a child receives can be counted the stories that he hears, and the attitudes that he then experiences, such as gratitude, awe, reverence, or the opposites. Children need some form of spiritual nourishment as well as physical. One has only to note the sigh of satisfaction after a child has listened to a suitable story. Above all children need a human relationship. Human beings are educated by other human beings. Love, warmth and human interest are vital to them. In themselves children have no guidance, and they need the help of understanding adults in order to find themselves; no impersonal machine is a substitute for the human factor.

Since the child is not a little adult, it is hopeless to try to teach him in an adult way, by logic and reason. We must seek the laws of childhood. Although every human being is an individual and shows individual characteristics, there is a fairly uniform general pattern of child development. Most human beings are conceived in the usual way. Pregnancy normally lasts nine months. At the age of one year or thereabouts most children begin to walk and talk. Between two and three they have a greater awareness of themselves as individuals, as is evidenced by the increasing use of the first person singular 'I'. In the course of time, the milk teeth drop out and permanent ones take their place. At six or seven the world of fantasy begins to fade. Puberty sets in at about thirteen.

The ages of six to seven and thirteen to fourteen are main staging posts in a child's development, with minor ones in between. We shall try to show how different forces manifest themselves at different periods, and how to work with these educationally. It is not a question of superimposing something on the child but of studying the laws of organic development, and thus working with nature.

The Infant (Birth to 7 years)

There is an obvious difference between the newly born

child lying in the cot, and the active, shouting, running and jumping youngster of five or six. Formal education is not concerned with the very young child but for the sake of completeness a few notes are included here on development in the early years. This period up to age seven has a uniform character, and the age of six or seven is marked by noticeable physical and mental development. Outwardly it is the time of the coming of the second teeth.

For those who can still experience some feeling of wonder and reverence the birth of a child is an event indeed. In the first days of his existence, particularly in his first hours, the child has a very strange look. He appears old and as if there is endless experience behind him. One almost has the impression that an epitome of the past has appeared. In the contemplative adult the very question of existence arises. Who is this personality? George Macdonald puts the question in one of his poems: 'Where did you come from, baby dear?'. The answer is: 'Out of the everywhere into here.' What parent cannot feel very near to another world at such a moment as that of birth?

In the first few months the baby sleeps a great deal. Now what is the significance of sleep? Normally, the human being has two levels of consciousness — waking and sleeping. We could also call sleeping, unconsciousness. What, then, is the difference between waking and sleeping? In waking, one is in possession of one's faculties; in sleeping one is not. We speak of a person being 'not all there', when his mind and body do not function together. In a similar sense the baby is 'not all there', and the process of growth is the process of getting 'there'; it takes some twenty or thirty years.

Even when awake a baby has not the same conscious awareness as the adult. When he wakes, he drinks and kicks, and then sleeps again if his bodily desires are satisfied. He presents a picture of primeval contentment, totally uncon-scious of his own innate forces. He is helpless, cannot stand, cannot walk, cannot feed himself. He is at the mercy of the understanding that a child of this period strives for is a sympathetic one, a 'feeling-understanding'. He cannot yet use definitions, but wants descriptions, preferably artistic ones.

If one observes children and grown-ups reacting to the same stimuli, say a concert, film or a race, one sees how the children react in a much more sympathetic way (using the word *sym-pathy* in the original sense of *feeling-with*). Children laugh, shout, jump, give vent to their feelings, whereas by comparison the adult is staid and reticent.

Gradually the child's mind during this period begins to be concerned with time and space. A little girl once asked me, 'Is it this morning or this afternoon?' Another typical question is, 'Is London in this world?' The child is not concerned with work as such. He is not concerned about where the next meal comes from. He is not 'thinking'. For him there is no difference between the aristocracy and the proletariat. Knowledge is not pigeon-holed. He does not expect to have to go to a scientist for an explanation of physical matter or to a biologist to learn about reproduction. Daddy or Mummy have all the answers and the adult is an authority. The child still sees the world as a unity.

Furthermore, the child in this period believes what he is told. He has faith in the good and accepts what is given him. Disillusionment has not yet set in. Curiosity and wonder are for him the gates of knowledge. He is interested in everything.

Although his reasoning powers are dormant, he is very much awake in the field of the imagination. I once had a child of seven in the car with me and she was fascinated by the speedometer needle. 'What's that?' she asked. As I was racking my brains to think up some stupid grown-up answer, she settled the problem herself. 'I know,' she said, 'it's a fairy's wand.' With that she was quite content.

The imaginative faculty is a force to be reckoned with. Threats, reason, logic cut little ice, but information given pictorially and appealing to the feeling element, goes home.

A child of this age is also naturally endowed with a feeling of awe and reverence. Even a dreamy child can be awakened and spurred to action by means of imaginative stories. How to make use of these powers educationally will be dealt with later.

The child between seven and fourteen has one further great need. It is the need for guidance. He is seeking his way into the world, tasting this and experimenting with that, but he has as yet no firm hold within himself or of himself. It is a fundamental need to have someone in authority over him, someone to direct, advise, guide, albeit in a personal, sympathetic way. That the child will sometimes rebel and reject the authority does not gainsay his need. He is testing his own powers, but he nevertheless needs the reassurance of the adult. It is an almost organic need, after the age of seven, to be instructed by adults as to what is good and right. The child wants to believe in the wisdom of the adult, and instinctively demands authority.

There are two minor milestones between the ages of seven and fourteen. These are at nine and twelve. Between seven and nine the memory of imitating or the desire to do so mingles with the desire for authority. The dreaminess gives way to a more conscious perception, and at the age of nine the child begins to take a real interest in the world around, and a certain egotistic development takes place. The child is becoming more conscious of himself as an individual but is not yet mature enough to make judgements or bear responsibility. For this reason a child of this age often appears to be cruel, self-centred, with an eye-for-an-eye and he-hit-me-first mentality.

From the ninth year onwards, the child will accept concepts, but from twelve onwards his nature demands them. Along with physical matuiity the power of thought is developing. The child now looks at the world and wants to learn about it from a reasoning point of view. It is no longer a matter that something just 'is'. The demand now is to know how and why. A tremendous new faculty is developing, the faculty of judgement. Only at twelve can the child really grasp cause and effect. Only at this age do thoughts take the place of pictures in the mind. The deepest questions now arise. 'Who am I?' 'How did the world begin?' 'What is God?' In the organic process of growth the wheels of the mind of man are beginning to turn.

SURVEY

Age	Nature of child	Inner Urge
4-6	Sensitive to, and dependent on, surroundings. Needs care, affection and protection.	Imitation. Will activity.
7-14	Features more defined. Walks with more grace and balance. In sympathy with the world. Understands via feelings and pictorial imagery. Has belief in the world and sees it as a unity.	Desire to learn. Needs authority.
At 9	Becomes more interested in the outer world and more conscious of self.	Wants to know more of the outer world.
At 12	Skeletal development. Questions relationship of self and world. Has ability to grasp cause and effect.	To attain understanding. How? Why?
14-18	Physical maturity. World interests. Individual perception and judgement. Develops stronger ego sense.	To argue, to reason, to question. Desire for independence.

Fourteen onwards

At the age of thirteen or fourteen the child, now becoming an adolescent, experiences a tremendous upheaval. He becomes aware of his body from a new angle. Physical maturity develops alongside a new mental awareness. Desires come up against opposition and authority loses its hold. Now the thinking processes come into their own. Laws of cause and effect can be understood. Individual powers of perception and judgement emerge. Interest awakens for the whole world, of which the opposite sex is part. Reasonable, logical explanations and appeals to reason are now needed. The adolescent can become an idealist, a hero, a crusader. He enjoys ideas, arguing and contradicting. He questions things. He questions his parents' authority, destiny, life itself. The adolescent can also suffer an inner loneliness. He is having to come to terms with himself. It is a difficult time; teachers must seek to guide but not to oppose.

At sixteen the young man or woman can understand the main facts of our modern civilisation, its discoveries and its achievements but he or she will also perceive the contradictions of modern life. Ideals of cooperation and brotherliness are expressed, while the manufacture and distribution of arms continues unabated; in some countries there are surpluses of food while thousands of people starve in others. It is thus all too easy to come to the conclusion that there is no real progress in human affairs, and that our civilisation is a veneer. At heart the young person is an idealist and these manifestations distress him. He wants to be assured that life is worthwhile and that there is some goal.

Because the basic searchings of the adolescent are often not satisfied in the modern world, there is a cry for distractions — sex, drugs, violence, demonstrations, religious or occult movements, 'back to nature' crusades.

At the ages of sixteen, seventeen, eighteen, the mind is asking for an explanation of life and the dead stones of modern materialistic science are insufficient. The mind has to be guided to an acceptable philosophy, and this is no easy task.

4

School Structure and Organisation

The nature of the child should tell us what to teach, and when and how to teach it, and how to organise our schools.

Schools naturally vary and it is not suggested here that they should become uniform. Every school differs according to its locality, according to its pupils and according to its staff. There are common characteristics in the nature of man, however, and so there will be a common pattern in schools.

The 'what', 'when' and 'how' of teaching will be considered in the following chapters. In this one the attempt is made to draw the logical conclusions on the structure of a school from what has already been described.

We spoke of the three distinct phases of child development — 0 to 6, 7 to 14, 14 onwards — and it would therefore seem a natural consequence to organise a school with three corresponding sections:-

The Infant School. Call this the nursery or kindergarten if you will. The age concerned would be from the time the child comes to school at four or five to the age of six. Two age groups may be necessary.

The Middle School. This would contain the children from age six to fourteen (second dentition to puberty), giving eight classes.

The Upper School. Here are the boys and girls from the

age of fourteen or fifteen to whatever is decided to be the school-leaving age. Educationally speaking, four years would be a good span.

The Infant School

We said that the small child is particularly influenced by his environment. One might think that the small child is unaware of his surroundings, and to the extent that he is not conscious of them, this is true. Observation shows, however, that the environment has a great influence on the small child. What sort of surroundings then should he have?

We know very well from personal experience that even as adults our surroundings affect us. We may be uncomfortable in a room of a certain colour. We may object to certain noises. Bosses or colleagues may get on our nerves. Such things are not conducive to a happy frame of mind or to our best achievement. We desire a pleasant, harmonious environment, but as adults we can and do cope with other conditions.

A pleasant, happy and harmonious environment is, however, an essential for the physical and mental welfare of the child. The question of the right home environment is one which we do not propose to deal with here, but the school environment must be carefully planned. A pleasant room is needed, of some artistic merit, with the right toys and material for work. A mature person is the best teacher. Academic qualifications are of far less importance than a natural understanding and aptitude for dealing with young children. Human warmth, and that is not meant in any sentimental sense, is far preferable to a degree. Patience and wisdom are required. These qualities are more likely to be found in a person of mature years. In the old days the children congregated around the grandmother. One does not doubt the fire, willingness, enthusiasm and capability of youth but in this particular instance, life experience is the best qualification.

The Middle School

It was said that guidance was a great need of the child at this period. He needs someone to direct and advise, an authority. The objection may be made that this is interfering in the growing independence of the child. Whoever advances such an argument has not observed child nature. Independence and a desire to have one's way are certainly there during these years, but as yet the child has no basis for judgement or experience, and longs for the authority of the adult. How often one hears children speaking disparagingly of a teacher who can't keep order, and praising the teacher who makes them work, although in the actual situation they may not express themselves so positively. The child of this period is easily swayed, and his stability and sense of security are fostered by having someone to make the decisions. In case we should be misunderstood, we are not advocating a harsh, semi-militaristic regime. The kind of authority meant is one combining firmness with kindness, and the person wielding it is at the same time the authority in the various branches of knowledge. The child still experiences the world as a unity and unity is expressed in a person. This person represents the world.

These basic needs of a child can be met in school by a good personal relationship with a teacher. In some schools children are forever on the move from one classroom to another and from one teacher to another. The knowledge given or received or the work done is scrappy in the extreme and there is a restlessness in the atmosphere which is disturbing and unproductive. Apart from these disadvantages few teachers have time to make proper contacts with the children. A specialist teacher, working through the school may have up to twenty different classes. At thirty to a class, that means six hundred children. Owing to present rapid turnover in staff, he may have them for merely a term or a year possibly. How can any human contact be made under such conditions? He cannot possibly call all the children to mind. The child has an endless succession of teachers delivering their special knowledge, but can form little personal relationship with them owing to their fleeting presence. His nature demands the opposite.

An arrangement to meet this need would be to give each class a teacher who not only marks the register but who spends a good deal of time with that particular class, and even keeps it over the whole period of years from the age of six to the age of fourteen. The objection can be raised that there may be cases of incompatibility between the teachers and a given child, but it should not be too difficult to transfer the child to a parallel class or even to another school. In any case, any teacher worth his salt would strive to overcome this. In this way the teacher is able to form a close association with a particular group of children, take a special interest in them, become their guide, philosopher and friend, and, even more important, the children have one person as the main representative of the adult world. It is an arrangement which contributes to their feeling of security and stability. They have some one who cares.

As noted above, the child sees the world as a unity. Therefore all main subjects should be in the hands of the class teacher. Main subjects could include English, mathematics, geography, history, and elementary science. If one person is handling these things, they can be better coordinated. The arrangement makes for greater economy in teaching; for instance, geography and history often overlap. In schools as they are at present, how many science teachers know what the history master is teaching? How much more sensible it would be to teach about the Industrial Revolution and the functioning of the steam engine at the same time.

With one person taking the chief subjects over a long period of time the child would be saved the continual change from one person's methods and attitudes to another's. It may be argued that change is a good thing and develops a flexibility in the mind. This is true, but up to fourteen a child needs stability to build a foundation and this is not achieved by continual changes. In any case, there would be some variation since, while one teacher took the main subjects, other teachers would take languages, gymnastics, handicrafts and whatever else is in the curriculum.

A further objection will be raised that one teacher cannot cope with all these main subjects. It is only valid so long as the right sort of people are not recruited as teachers and trained properly. Training used to be for two years, now it is three. Why not extend it, if necessary? Good education will pay dividends.

There is also another immense benefit to be derived from the one teacher taking many subjects over a period of years, and that is that he himself cannot get stale. Think of one teacher taking the same subject with the same age group for thirty years. How many times will he repeat himself? How tired he will be of saying the same thing over again. By contrast a class teacher in the above sense must keep his mind active and alert — to the immense benefit of the pupils.

In present secondary school time-tables there is all too often a change of teacher and a change of subject. With what result? Let us think of a car ride sightseeing. One can see an enormous number of things but one has no time to absorb. If one impression follows another too quickly the result is superficiality. If a child is really to learn, it needs time to digest, particularly if the will is to be involved. The mind needs time to penetrate a subject. As one hour in the morning is worth two in the afternoon, at least as far as brain activity is concerned, it follows that the more important intellectual work should be done first thing. Children and the teacher are obviously much fresher in the morning and possibly very much otherwise in the afternoon, when digesting their good school dinner. It is, therefore, obvious that if we are to have morning and afternoon school, there must be a change of activity.

Recent research has shown how efficiency varies throughout the day. If school begins at nine o'clock, then a peak of efficiency is reached between ten and eleven. This decreases to a minimum between one and two. There is a rise towards three, followed by a decline.

The obvious arrangement of the school day is thus to take intellectual subjects in the morning, and arts, crafts and activities in the afternoon. The order of the day should be: conscious learning, then something of a routine nature which requires practice but less active thinking, followed by an activity. Undoubtedly there would be some difficulty in making a time-table but this should not deflect us from recognising the best arrangement.

One possible objection is that tests show a child to be incapable of concentrating on one subject for more than twenty minutes. This is simply not true. If a child is bored, of course, his attention will wander long before ten minutes are up, but a subject can also be taught in an interesting way. It can be studied from various points of view. It can be talked about by the teacher, written about by the pupils, illustrated, possibly acted. To use a well-worn phrase in modern education — the child must be involved.

If there is a long period available the teacher can get the class into the right mood. Let us consider for a moment the conditions under which some children, especially those in a city, come to school. Perhaps they have travelled a great distance. They have dodged traffic and have been exposed to all sorts of stimulating and exciting sense impressions. Are they in the mood to settle down and study? The teacher may have to do a little preliminary work to order and calm the children before giving the actual lesson, and this takes time. It might be possible to use the school assembly for such a purpose if school assemblies were not so often a hotch-potch of religious worship, notices and injunctions. It would be more effective to have a little chat, singing, recitation, or music in the more intimate atmosphere of the single classroom.

For the same reason that time is needed, it would be a good thing for one subject to be studied not only for a fairly long period each day, but each day for several weeks. This would give depth and allow concentration. An objection to this may be that if a concentrated period is taken for one subject, a fair length of time will have to elapse before the matter is taken up again, and most of it will therefore be forgotten. One might respond by asking how much is remembered under present conditions, anyway? The experts tell us 2%. There are certain things which must be practised as a daily routine, such as spelling or arithmetic tables, and even if only a few minutes daily are spent on them, they will stick in the memory. But in subjects like history or geography, it is true that a great deal will be forgotten.

Nevertheless, a good case can be made out even for forgetting. Everyone needs time to digest. After a meal some hours elapse before the food is absorbed into the system. The argument applies equally well to learning. This book, for example, is being written in spasms, a period of intense writing, then a pause. During the pause new thoughts evolve even if one is not thinking of the matter. So it is with children learning. They can become satisfied and it is then healthy to make a change. The matter has gone from the conscious memory, but it is not lost. It is being digested and incorporated in the mental system. With a little effort and stimulation it can in some measure be recalled. It is probably a good idea to recapitulate all subjects which have been taken in periods at the end of the term or at the end of the year.

The child lives in rhythms. The baby wants his meals and sleeping times regularly, and such arrangements are usually considered the healthiest. We know how upsetting broken rhythms can be. The child, more than the adult, is affected by seasons and the weather. Teachers have no control over these but they do know that discipline is more difficult in summer than in winter and that quite a different mood enters the class on a stormy day. Why not, then, counterbalance these disturbing influences and meet the child's need for ordered rhythmical activity by organising his work accordingly? That is to say, arrange the timetable as already indicated but let it also bring the same things at the same hour daily.

Practically this would work out as follows. There would be a main lesson daily of some one-and-a-half or two hours. After the main lesson there might be something a little relaxing, say music, singing, recorder playing, religion or stories of some sort, followed by a language lesson or a practice period. In the afternoon would come practical activities, gymnastics, games or sport. There is usually some controversy over the length of a lesson. Except for the main lesson, three quarters of an hour seems a good average, with of course, double periods for those subjects, like art, which demand it.

The question of school hours, too, is one which is worth investigation. Quantity is not to be equated with quality. Some economy of time would be achieved through the coordinated main lesson. To give a good main lesson calls for good solid preparation on the part of the teacher; therefore he should teach fewer hours. For the child who has received something substantial, fewer hours in school may be beneficial, or at least involve less sitting on a school bench, which is not a very natural place for a child, anyway. It might be a good idea to follow the German pattern in this respect. In Germany children in the lower school classes have morning school only, consisting of perhaps three or four lessons, and no one would suggest that the Germans are less learned than we are.

The timetable would look like this approximately, with changes day by day except for the main lesson which would change only every three or four weeks:-

9-11	Main subject — English, mathematics, geography, history, science, etc.
11-11.45	Music, singing, recorders, religion, story.

11.45-12.30   French, German or other language, practise
               period.
                       Break
2-3.30   Handwork, craftwork, sports, excursions.

If the younger children are in school for a shorter period,
then the afternoon activities are incorporated in the morning
work. If necessary, older pupils could have their day
extended. There are naturally all sorts of practical difficulties if all children are not at school for all the time, but
that should not deter one from expressing an ideal.

Homework is often a knotty problem. Obviously the older
a child is, the more work can be demanded. The idea of
homework often arouses antipathy but the aim should be so
to arouse interest that the child is happy to do some or even
ask for it.

The difficulty of one teacher taking a group of children
for most subjects for eight years, has already been referred
to. It should be made clear that the class teacher does not
take *all* subjects but only the main ones. Specialist teachers
take their own subjects. While class teachers are taking their
main lessons, the specialist teachers can be doing their stint
in the upper school since the class teacher arrangement no
longer applies here.

Fourteen onwards

At this age children kick over the traces. They will have
made attempts before but this is the final effort and it is the
time when the adult must begin to loosen the reins and
finally drop them. Growing adolescents already begin to feel
themselves as adults, to feel their own weight, recognise
themselves as individuals and cock a snook at authority.
Their minds are branching out in all directions and their
nature now not only seeks, but also demands, ideas and
explanations. Only the expert in his field can satisfactorily
measure up to this probing. Whereas, up to now, the human
element has been paramount, i.e. not the knowledge but the

personality of the teacher has been of prime importance, it is now the other way round. It is thus logical that from the age of fourteen upwards the instruction should be in the hands of specialists. A succession of personalities now also helps growth.

Other factors still hold good. Main lessons in blocks of several weeks allow a proper study in depth; intellectual work in the morning, activities later in the day as far as possible.

No reference has so far been made to the age at which children should first attend school or the age at which they should leave. As already noted, the right time to begin formal education is between six and seven, the time of the second dentition. But factors other than educative ones play into the right age for pre-school, and the leaving age. On the basis of the nature of the human being, can such ages be determined?

The early years belong to the home and the mother and it seems natural that the invisible threads which bind mother and child should only gently be severed. At some age the child feels safe enough to sally forth and this is usually between three and four. After the age of four the child needs social relationships and this then would be the time to attend a nursery or kindergarten, perhaps mornings only, where two years can well be spent before starting in the first class of the regular school. In some cases a child might not be ready until five and although a little persuasion might be in place there should be no compulsion.

With changing economic conditions and more insight into the needs of young people the school-leaving age is being gradually advanced. The powers of thinking and judgement only awaken at fourteen so that even at sixteen it is too early to be cast out into the world. The adolescent needs time, after his conceptual faculties have awakened, to absorb world culture, world history and all aspects of world development. He also needs time to test and develop his own powers while still being partially protected and guided, so that his launching into the world is a gradual process. Four years in which to make the transition is not too much so that eighteen appears as a reasonable school-leaving age.

The objection will be raised that in present circumstances there will be many students who will not benefit from longer education and who may actively resent it. This in no way invalidates the argument. It merely emphasises the failure of our present methods of education. At fourteen many children are school-weary for the simple reason that they have been miseducated in their younger years. Through pictorial imagery their interests and minds must be awakened and stimulated in the early years. Perhaps the ideas contained in this book will provide a remedy for the fed-up-at-fourteen malaise.

It will also be argued that not all children are academically-minded and that eighteen is too late for children whose future lies in practical work. The solution to this is to combine apprenticeship with school life, not as it is sometimes done by day release classes or evening classes, but by bringing workshops to the school. At the age of sixteen it is fairly clear to which activity young people incline. From this age onward then, let all pupils take part in a general cultural education, but arrange practical courses for the practical-minded–courses which will lead to the necessary certificates for carpentry, engineering, plumbing, etc., and courses suitable for the girls.

Naturally, administrative difficulties will arise but in the final instance what is educationally right must be administratively possible, not the other way round.

That such an arrangement is feasible and practicable is proved by the fact that it is carried out at Nuremberg's Rudolf Steiner School. Here *all* senior pupils take part in lessons dealing with general culture first thing in the morning. Then they split, academics in one direction, practical workers in another. The school can offer both tuition to university entrance and complete apprenticeship training leading to the approved certificates.

The folly of letting education be predetermined by examinations is widely recognised. If there is to be an examination, then this should be on what has been learnt for its educational value. In this respect some arrangements in Germany again can set us an example. In Hanover a school can set up its own syllabus and the pupils are then set examinations by their teachers in conjunction with government examiners. Something similar is allowed in Hamburg. Obviously then the school can teach what it considers to be of educational value and not merely whatever helps pupils to pass an examination.

It goes without saying that all artificial segregation is harmful. The child is part of a community. There should therefore be no distinctions of class in the school. Doctors', craftsmens' and labourers' children should be sitting side-by-side, mutually giving and receiving. The social problem will never be solved if children are segregated socially. In a multiracial society like Hawaii, where there is no effective racial prejudice, children of all races and mixtures play happily side-by-side. The state governor may be of European extraction, the Minister of Education, Japanese, the Chief Justice, Chinese. It is a very happy community.

Only a recognition of common humanity will solve the social problem. Preaching about brotherhood and equality will get nowhere. Men are not equal. Out of a class of children perhaps one will become Prime Minister and another a bricklayer. Each in his way contributes to the community and each has the right to absorb as much of our cultural inheritance as he can.

There will always be social distinctions. By mixing the social strata we are not aiming at an egalitarian society but a society where every human being is valued as such.

So too, both sexes should be in school together. Nobody disputes the physical differences or the mental and intellectual disparities. *Vive la différence!* This is life. By and large, girls have a better comprehension of what is religious and artistic. Boys perhaps on the whole understand material things better. But it is just such differentials which make for fruitful cooperation.

The same arguments apply also to staff. Men and women should be working together as teachers so that the pupils get the benefit of both elements.

Further, all ages should be under one roof. There are immense advantages to be gained in a unified school. Do our administrators ever assess the loss when children change schools? The nursery should perhaps be a little on one side so as to avoid the worst of the hurly-burly, but even here, from a social point of view, it is good to let the little ones at least see the older children and thus give them a preview of things to come. It is also good for the older ones to look back and see the path along which they have travelled.

In the same line of thought and depending on circumstances, a special class for the retarded should be instituted within the school. There is some movement towards this in modern education. Special classes are being arranged for slow learners. Whether this is quite the answer is questionable. As far as possible, backward or even maladjusted children should remain within a normal community. It would be an excellent thing if the slow child could receive extra coaching or assistance in a special class, and eventually return to his normal class.

Many children today suffer from some psychological disturbance. It would, therefore, be useful to have a doctor, preferably versed in psychology or psychiatry, on the staff. These experts are available today but are remote figures. 'On the staff' in this context means as a teacher, as a colleague; one who is readily available on a day-to-day basis as part of the concern.

What of the headmaster and staff relationships? Now the whole purpose of running a school is to educate children,

and all teachers are *in loco parentis,* being expected to look
after children as a parent would. It is a corporate responsibility. Loyalty is to the children, not to another person.

What is needed in place of a head master is a staff working
together. Thus everybody is responsible for school and
children. This does not mean that everybody does everything or that everybody's business is nobody's business. It
does mean that the corporate body of teachers takes matters
into its own hands, appoints a chairman for meetings,
delegates responsibilities to its various members, and
regularly discusses not only organisation and administration
but also teaching methods and invididual children.

Thus all teachers would be brought in. They would feel
that this is their school. There would be mutual support. The
present scramble for positions of special responsibility would
cease. There would be equal pay for equal work and there
would be a stable staff.

The physical appearance of the school building and
classrooms is important. In earlier ages buildings spoke
beauty themselves, as, for example, the Greek temples and
the Gothic cathedrals. In our present age buildings are
purpose-built. They are not always unpleasant to look at but
whether the building houses a school or a factory is not
always easy to say unless one reads the notice board. Since
environment has an effect on everybody and especially on
children, one may be forgiven for thinking that a school
building with some grace would have a beneficial formative
effect on the pupils. The value of the human relationship as
part of the environment is well recognised. Children need
love, warmth, interest and guidance, an atmosphere which
teachers must provide. Why not also a building which
welcomes the child instead of a soul-less series of cubistic
blocks?

In the classrooms themselves, where children sit for such
long periods, surely a little beauty is in place. Perhaps an
artist could design a layout, including desks, colouring and

blackboard positioning so that a more friendly tone enters.

Thus there are many improvements which could be made in organisation. These are: the threefold structure of the school, the concentrated main lesson, the rhythm of the day. Brain work should be done in the morning periods. New staffing arrangements are desirable. Buildings and general surroundings could be more artistic.

5

What to Teach

When a child comes to school he may show this or that talent. Later he may develop others. He may have some latent gift which remains so because it is never awakened. The teacher may not discover it. A boy of nine may want to be a pilot and have a flair for mechanical objects. Perhaps he also has a talent for music but, being 'brainy' he gets into a school environment where music and the arts are considered of minor importance; thus his talent could remain dormant. He leaves school, receives whatever further education is allotted to him, passes his examinations and goes to work. He marries, has family responsibilities and, too late, he discovers his musical capacity. It is impossible now to change and a sense of frustration is the result.

One school of philosophy explains the world as something which has arisen as the result of pure chance, and man is at the end of the line. Another tells us that the world has evolved with man as its central theme, its reason for existence. Whatever philosophy or science may have to say on the point, the fact remains that man is connected with the world in a multitude of ways. His bones, flesh and physical body are composed of physical substance. His nourishment comes from the earth whose products are in turn dependent on light and warmth which come from outer space. His time is reckoned by sun, moon and stars. There is no branch of knowledge which in some way does not concern him. If, therefore, we put the question as to what should be taught, the answer is virtually 'everything'.

The child's aim is to become an adult, cognisant of the world. The child is neither blasé nor indifferent. All the world is interesting and he wants to know all about it. Curiosity and wonder are the beginning of knowledge. However, we must not fall into the error of thinking that elementary education means simplifying adult knowledge. It was said above that the child is not a small edition of the adult. He has different powers of comprehension and he has a different mental constitution. What is taught, therefore, and how it is taught, must be scaled to this. Simplified explanations are not the proper order of things. He needs knowledge and experience commensurate with his state of mind.

There is something more that the child needs. He wants to unfold his own powers. He must experience and eventually reason and his experience must be as wide as possible. Therefore, if a man or woman is to have a comprehensive understanding of the world and if all his or her talents are to be awakened, the school syllabus must include all subjects.

There is a further point. In an age where the boundaries of knowledge are continually expanding, where Europe and the world as a whole are striving for economic unity, where America is on Britain's doorstep, where the welfare of all peoples has become a subject of consideration, there is no place for narrow parochial thinking. To develop wide interests, a broad mind, and a universal understanding is a social act.

These are fundamental matters both for the individual and the community. They are taken care of if education is sufficiently liberal. Let us make a list of the things that we consider a moderately educated person should know something about: the pupil's native language and literature; world literature; mathematics in all its branches; foreign languages; physics; chemistry; natural history (plants and animals); world geography; world history; peoples and races; physiology; politics and civics; first aid; arts (painting, sculpture, architecture, music); religion.

The list is not intended to be exhaustive. We must get away from the idea of studying a certain number of subjects to pass an examination to the idea of education to one's own potential and one's own breadth of vision.

We must keep the purpose of education under continual review. Amassing knowledge, and thereby, we hope, acquiring understanding, is satisfactory to one facet of man's nature, but another is that he requires some physical activity and creative outlet. Walking, tennis, golf will perhaps satisfy some adult desires. The more adventurous will opt for such things as mountaineering, underwater swimming or skiing. But there is also the urge to be creative; hence the number of hobbies — gardening, painting, sailing, even repairing the car.

So besides dispensing knowledge the school must also stimulate and prepare for an intelligent use of these other faculties. Under this heading can be listed: practice of the arts (painting, drawing, wood or stone carving, singing, drama, playing an instrument); handicrafts of all types (weaving, carpentry, metalwork, basket-making); farming and gardening; sport.

Again the list could no doubt be extended and it is not claimed that all these activities would be feasible in school. Yet the general principle holds good. The statement 'to teach everything' must of course, be interpreted in an 'embryonic' sense. We cannot teach all languages. We cannot teach all sciences. We cannot teach all of anything, but we can introduce and stimulate interest in most things. Nor do we mean that all the various subjects must be given at once. Indeed it would be difficult to teach higher mathematics, for example, to a six-year-old. Once the stages of human development, as enumerated earlier, are recognised, it becomes fairly obvious what subjects should be taken and when. We do not grow oranges and bananas in a soil and climate unsuited to them. Subjects and methods must accord with child nature.

From the state of minimal consciousness of the small child to the full waking consciousness of the mature adult is a long way. The child should not be shocked into awareness by too much factual knowledge or demand for skills. The world is still a little vague to the child and the path is from story via simile to knowledge. The child's mind can be led and encouraged, but should not be forced. Let us always bear in mind organic development.

Arguments put forward above as to the number of school hours suitable for a child, apply also to subjects. Let the introduction to school work be gradual on both a quantitative and a qualitative basis. But it must also be borne in mind that the child should learn widely so that it has a richness of knowledge and a foundation for judgement later. In this chapter the attempt is made to suggest 'what' should be learnt at the different ages; the 'how' of teaching is the subject of the next.

The years in the nursery can be considered as pre-school years. The children there learn social relationships; they are introduced to painting, drawing, modelling, games. They become accustomed to certain routines, but formal schooling only begins at six.

For his own benefit as well as for the purpose of fitting into the community, a child must acquire a good knowledge of the mother tongue. This is in so many respects the key to all further learning and must be practised assiduously. At what age the child should learn to read and write is open to argument but it is an accepted convention that these faculties must be acquired. The child has already learnt to speak without any direct tuition and the natural process is to extend this. That is to say, the child should learn to listen and to retell what he has heard. Language is essentially a spoken art. In a sense it dies when committed to paper.

It is postulated that the child will be listening to well

spoken English, or whatever is his native tongue. The onus
is on the teacher. Listening and retelling is splendid exercise
for mind and tongue. The proper material for this age is
stories. Grimms' and Andrew Lang's fairy tales are particularly suitable as they provide the right form of 'nourishment'. One can also tell simple nature stories which are
descriptive pictures without scientific bias or explanatory
intent. Useful, too, are simple stories of the world around so
that the child gains closer contact with his environment.

With regard to reading and writing, one school of thought
advocates the learning of these with great intensity as early as
possible and another thinks them of far less importance in
the early years. If one considers that these faculties have only
become general possessions relatively late in history, one gets
the right perspective. It also helps if one considers the nature
of the young child. At six the child is a lively active being with
a great impulse to run and skip and there is something
contrary to nature to see him confined to a classroom and
laboriously practising letters with a pen or pencil stuck
between his fingers. By the same token, concentration on the
printed word seems very confining. If these things must be
taught, let us not lay too great a stress on them in the early
years. There is much for the child to learn and to experience
without these achievements. There is, for instance, the whole
sphere of artistic activity — speaking, singing, painting,
modelling, drawing, acting; there are practical activities like
handwork, gardening and games. Even foreign languages
can be learnt to some extent and a great deal of number
work and study of shapes — call it arithmetic and geometry if
you will — can be done without ever writing down or seeing a
figure or formula.

In fact it may be that the actual visible form is a hindrance
to imaginative activity. Most children already have some
experience of the relationship between numbers when they
come to school. It is therefore a question of their becoming
conscious of the relationship between numbers and processes,
i.e. the four rules. Rhythmic counting helps, particularly if

accompanied by action. As children learn easily by rote, moreover, there is no harm in their beginning to learn the multiplication tables, even if they are not fully understood. Children often want to learn things by heart and the tables can be learnt equally well along with rhymes, poems and songs. When it is deemed time to introduce the letters, the written symbols for numbers can also be learnt. In practice, most of the children will already be acquainted with these.

It sometimes happens that a given child has little or no feeling or skill for mathematics, and is therefore left to fend for himself in this respect. This is a wrong attitude, since mathematics is a very important subject. One should never give up trying to teach it. There is a certain progression in mathematics and geometry which makes them suitable for all ages, unlike, say, basic studies on animals or plants which are suitable for one particular age.

In relation to the four aims of education given in chapter two, the acquisition of mathematical skills is obviously essential — everyone has to be able to deal with number and form. As to social relationships, mathematics is a realm where all must agree. People may vary in opinion as to whether the sea is blue or green, blue-green or green-blue, but in mathematics there is only one answer — $2 + 2 = 4$ — always. There is universal agreement. In the solving of problems or in the contemplation and working out of geometrical metamorphoses there is for some people the same satisfaction as in painting or acting. There is a spirit of discovery. Enthusiasm is engendered.

As for the fourth aim of education there are many aspects of mathematics which further spiritual development. One can be led to ponder on the qualitative values of, for example, 1, 7 or 12; what is 'oneness'? One thus realises universal laws; space goes by twelves, time by sevens.

Learning mathematics is the development of logical thought applied to physical tasks. It leads to imaginative thought, e.g. visualising forms which do not exist in the physical world but only in the world of ideas. There are external verities in mathematics. Was it not Plato who said, 'God mathematizes'? In comprehending mathematics the individual feels himself to be part of the whole universe.

In the past the typical English attitude to learning foreign languages was to expect the foreigners to learn English, which in fact they did — and still do. But as international relations grow closer and not *all* foreigners speak or write English, it is perhaps incumbent upon us to bestir ourselves. There are, moreover, other advantages in learning a foreign tongue other than the purely utilitarian. Learning a foreign tongue develops a flexibility of mind, gives a different viewpoint, and is often a help in understanding one's own language.

Children of six have already learnt their mother tongue simply by listening and repeating. They try out sounds and by some subtle process connect certain sounds with objects or activities. So why not make use of this faculty and plasticity and start learning foreign languages at six? It is certainly the easiest time at which to acquire a good accent.

Just which languages to learn is a matter of choice but languages of different character should be chosen to enlarge the experience. It would be better to take French and German rather than French and Spanish. Perhaps Russian should find its way into the curriculum.

The child at this age often cannot sing in tune but a beginning of a musical education can be made by singing simple songs and learning the recorder.

Those clumsy young fingers often want something to do and they can well be engaged in improving their dexterity. For this, knitting can be recommended and since we are thinking of educational aspects, let no eyebrows be raised at the thought of boys knitting. If it is accepted that knitting or something similar is a good healthy educational activity, then let us not deprive the boys of it on account of some sentimental idea of what properly belongs to the distaff side. The boys themselves will work with interest and enthusiasm.

In the matter of creative artistic work — self-expression —

painting will perhaps have pride of place. Painting with free-flowing water colours, whereby no attempt is made to depict objects, will afford the child the greatest satisfaction. One could almost let the child play with the colours (in the first place the three primary ones), and let him 'discover'. Let him experience how blue looks by the side of yellow, or how yellow looks surrounded by red, or what happens when blue and yellow merge. Eventually he will paint something, look at it and then declare it to be a picture of something totally unrecognisable by the adult but giving proof positive that a creative imaginative mind is at work. Drawing and modelling are further suitable activities so long as they are kept within the realm of free imagination and attempts to copy objects are not encouraged.

Religious instruction, as far as young children are concerned, is a matter of awakening feelings of wonder, awe, reverence, gratitude. There are many opportunities for this in the ordinary course of teaching, but if there is to be a religious lesson, then let it be a story or an anecdote, real or imaginary which will stir the feelings in that way. Better still, let the story arouse the feeling that there is some unseen creative power in the universe. Stories of fairies and gnomes do this very well. No explanation or pointing out of morals should be undertaken.

Thus for the first year, ages six to seven, we have: English in various forms — speaking, listening, reciting, reading, writing; arithmetic; two foreign languages; music — singing, recorder playing and listening to good music; artistic work — painting, drawing, modelling; craftwork — knitting or similar work; general knowledge; religion; games.

For the second year, work continues in a similar pattern. Legends and fables, still without explanations, take the place of fairy stories. The scope of general knowledge is widened. Under this heading is meant stories about plants and animals and everyday stories of the world. Free geometrical forms can be practised, merely for the pleasure and the experience and not for intellectual analysis or explanation. The child, living in a rather vague 'unearthly' world, really wants to come to grips with reality. In drawing geometrical forms he is experiencing the harmony in which he lives but at the same time he is aware of what he is doing. This is then a stage of consciousness. It is a slight awakening.

In telling stories or relating incidents, one finds that the good is pleasing and the bad displeasing. An emphasis on this will serve to build a moral sense as the terms right and wrong have, as yet, little meaning.

It has already been noted that the age of nine brings a change. The child becomes more awake. While up to this age the environment has interested him in a dreamy sort of way, now his questions take a different turn and the interest shifts to the desire for a more exact picture.

The subjects already mentioned will, therefore, be continued but with special features being emphasised to meet the child's needs. In English, for instance, writing, reading and speaking having been learnt in some measure, attention should be turned to the structure of the language, the bones, so to speak, the grammar, and a beginning can be made with the parts of speech and the parts of a sentence.

In the matter of mathematics the children will be interested in practical matters. It is the time for all sorts of exercises in practical usage within the bounds of their experience, but always reaching out a little further. This is the time to learn the money system, the weights and measures and all sorts of problems dealing with these. It is a matter for some regret and an educational loss that we are moving towards the soul-less decimal system.

The child at this age, nine, will be developing a feeling of independence and will want to do things by himself. This is natural and should be encouraged. Thus, as well as dealing with all sorts of practical problems, practical work which can be done individually should be undertaken with ruler, compass and set-square.

As story material particularly suited to this age one could make use of the Old Testament stories. The child of nine and ten needs and expects authority, and requires praise or reproach according to his deserts in order to fortify his own moral fibre. Many stories of the Old Testament provide an objective picture of the child's own development. The relationship of Jehovah to the Jews parallels the child's own experience with authority. 'Thou shalt or thou shalt not.' There is a short essay by Lessing entitled 'The Education of the Human Race', where this idea of the Jews being treated as children, in an age before humanity as a whole reached a further stage of maturity, is advanced.

The approach of the child's mind to practical things should now be supported by all sorts of practical activities and descriptions of activities, particularly human occupations. If these are taking place in the neighbourhood, so much the better. It is excellent to be able to see practical work being done — farming, gardening, building, mining, quarrying. In the city it may be difficult to find some of these though usually there is some building taking place or holes are being dug to take one or other of the numerous contrivances — cables, sewers, etc. — belonging to our civilisation.

There is a difference, of course, between merely observing or being told, and participation. In spite of the difficulties one may find in obtaining it, the real experience, participation, is by far the more rewarding. Therefore, as far as possible, children should engage in practical tasks like mixing mortar or concrete, bricklaying, ploughing and planting, cooking. At this age it is not so much a question of acquiring the skill, or of experience for the sake of gaining knowledge, as of fostering appreciation of human labour and of getting away from the academic other-worldly atmosphere of the classroom.

With the gradual loss of the easy-flowing harmonious rhythmic movements of early childhood comes also a different awareness of one's own body. While games will have provided sufficient physical activity up to now, a more consciously formed movement is now called for — hence this is the time to introduce elementary gymnastics. Also, handwork should now become more exacting with the tendency towards the practical. Knitted woollen caps, jumpers or tea-cosies, for example, could be made. Similarly, the painting should now take on a more definite form although still from creative imagination and not based on copying. Drawing can be undertaken using a technique of shading with crayons or coloured pencils whereby an object in the picture evolves and is not already predetermined by an outline.

Musical instruction, which, up to now, has been singing, recorder playing, or musical appreciation, can now include the beginnings of staff notation. In religion, stories of the saints provide the right sort of material.

This is then the sort of syllabus suitable for children of nine to ten: English, as before but with grammar added; arithmetic — practical problems, weights and measures; two foreign languages, and a start on reading and writing them; music, as before but with staff notation added; artistic work, as before but with more form; craftwork; general knowledge; religion — stories of saints or similar; games; gymnastics; special periods of study on practical work with participation where possible — housebuilding, farming, gardening; stories from the Old Testament as history.

We have reached and passed the tenth birthday. The trend towards a more practical view of life and the diversification of what earlier was one world, continues. New tasks in English can be undertaken in connection with syntax and punctuation. Business letters can be written as well as the usual run of compositions and summaries. With the unified view of the world breaking up into subjects, the learning of fractions is in the right place here. So is reading staff notation as well as further efforts with the recorder. For the musically gifted a special instrument can now be chosen, although individual tuition lies outside the general scope of class work. Greater attention should he given to exactness in handwork.

Learning about the immediate surroundings is pursued further, now not as stories but as knowledge. We have here the beginnings of geography, history, geology, biology. A study of the immediate neighbourhood should be made. Why did this particular village or town come into existence at this spot? How has it grown? What are the geographical features? What do the inhabitants do? What trees and plants grow in the district? What animals live there?

The child of ten stands opposite nature in a more objective way. He begins to feel himself as something belonging to and yet apart from nature. He is anxious to learn more about himself. He still needs pictorial imagery for his understanding and therefore one of the best ways of teaching him something about the human being is to make a study of 'Man and Animal'. This is not in any sense intended as a study of biology or zoology. Its purpose is to point out the essential human qualities by showing the differences between man and animal.

(Each animal species presents an evolutionary development which is less marked in man. In one sense the animal has achieved greater perfection but this is also its limitation; it is more perfect in one particular direction. The human being is less perfect, or less 'finished', but more harmonious and flexible. The animal uses its paw as a tool. By contrast the human hand is so formed that it is not itself a tool, but can hold and use a tool. Only man has the capacity of using his physical organism in a consciously directed way.)

The bustling, jostling nature of the ten-year-old can be paralleled in stories by relating the boisterous action tales of Norse mythology. These provide nourishment for the mind and accord with the child's development. The final story of the crashing of the rainbow bridge and the destruction of Valhalla parallel the child's experience in coming out of his dream world on to the earth.

In foreign languages, grammar can now be studied intensively, the groundwork having been prepared through the mother tongue. Reading, writing, listening and speaking will obviously be continued. Where appropriate the classical languages can be introduced.

Parallel with the study of grammar, the introduction of a more conscious element into the gymnastics, and the developing practical outlook, should go instruction in music theory. As the process of individualisation continues, two-part singing, or two-part playing on the recorder can be practised, progressing to three-and four-part items. Where talent and opportunity are available the playing of individual instruments should be further encouraged.

In gymnastics, exercises are required to bring about a greater awareness of the body and to develop courage. Artistic work can be related to other instruction. Religious experience can still be provided by stories but another approach would be to give biographies or partial biographies whereby the young mind is stirred through learning of the deeds and destinies of other people.

Thus the syllabus for this year (age 10) would now include a period on man and animal, and stories from Norse mythology.

The child of eleven has a growing understanding of time and space. His mind is probing and analysing. He has not yet achieved the power of logical thought but is nevertheless thinking. He feels differently about himself to what he does about the rest of the world. His natural capacity for learning and working is, of course, increasing.

To meet these conditions the pattern of work already detailed is followed but with additions. In English, direct and indirect speech should be practised and the reporting or summarising of what has been heard or read. What was a study of the neighbourhood in a general way now breaks down into various subjects such as geography, history, study of plants. The geography is extended to the county or country, depending on location. In history, in order to give an idea of the changing pattern of man's life and outlook one goes back to the ancient civilisations and comes up to the present in sequence. Thus the great cultures are passed in review — India, Persia, Egypt, Greece and Rome.

An elementary study of man and animal was made in the previous year, now the interest is directed towards the plant kingdom. The child of eleven is still endeavouring to come to terms with his own relationship with the world, and it is here that the study of the plant world can be of help. Again, it is not a question of a scientific study but a matter of appreciation of the plant between heaven and earth. It can be explained how the root belongs to the earth, and is of the nature of the earth. The flower is ethereal and partakes of the qualities of air and light. the green leaves form the connection and balance. There are similes to be drawn with the human being himself. A further thought is that in the plant world, nature expresses herself in a multitude of ways, yet it is one world which the plants manifest. The metamorphosis of the plant, in the Goethean sense, can be an educative factor and it is interesting to find geometrical designs in the plant world pointing almost to a mathematical concept.

Arithmetic will consist of further practice in all the matters already introduced, plus decimal fractions.

At the age of twelve comes a minor turning point. The child's movements lose their rhythm and grace and become angular and awkward. The limbs seem a burden and the child does not know what to do with them. It is a sign of a further step into the physical world. It is the obvious time when the sciences will appeal to the pupil. He will now begin to have the necessary comprehension for science in its pure form. Therefore we can now introduce physics and chemistry proper. This is the year for a beginning with practical gardening which can be continued for the next two years in order that the cycle of growth may be properly experienced.

It is also time for woodcarving, woodwork or other practical tasks. These are the new subjects relative to the chronological age.

The age of twelve is also one of practical realism. Not only will dynamics and mechanics be studied with natural interest but also law and the relationships between man and man. It is, therefore, appropriate at this age to learn about the Romans. The earlier periods have already been touched upon, mainly through myth and legend, as these are more appropriate for the earlier years. Now we have greater realism and history proper.

Beginning then with Rome at the age of twelve, the course of history to present times can be dealt with until about the age of fifteen. Geography will extend to a study of the whole earth and include the solar system and mathematical geography. Geology can be introduced.

Mathematics is continued generally, work consisting of percentages, discount, squaring, cubing. A start can be made with algebra, and, in geometry, with theorems. The so-called 'new maths' contains many elements which are not new but which have acquired a new terminology. Freehand geometrical drawing and the completion of symmetrical figures (now called reflections) have already been mentioned. As a new awareness develops at twelve, it is the age for the practise of geometrical exercises such as reflections, and rotations, shears and enlargements. Through our weights and measures we are already familiar with different number systems, i.e. others not based on ten, e.g inches, feet, etc. This would be the age to deal with such number systems.

At twelve, practical things should be made in handwork such as shirts, blouses, toys, or other useful objects. To be given a block of wood and tools, and then to form the block in the way one has in mind is a marvellous exercise for the will.

New subjects for the twelve-year-olds thus include physics, chemistry, woodwork and history proper.

No great changes are called for during the thirteenth year, but about the age of fourteen there comes not only the physical development of puberty but also a great change in mentality.

Up to now the child has been absorbing knowledge as well as acquiring skills and these processes will continue in ever greater measure. But now something more is required. The mind is now reaching out, enquiringly and questioningly. There are rumblings in the dark recesses of the subconscious. Who am I? Why is there human existence? What is the end of all things? It is basically a search for self.

In the normal way what do we give adolescents? For those going on to higher education, we give a more intensive dose of chosen subjects; for the intellectually slow, perhaps practical work or just something to keep them quiet! What adolescents really need, however, are other people's ideas on the world. It is the fashion to have a discussion and get opinions from the pupils, but it is futile to do this if a substantial basis of knowledge has not already been laid. When the deepest questions arise in the minds of adolescents, the most rewarding thing is to give them the views of philosophers, that is to say, to give them spiritual food for their own digestion.

Apart from the normal school subjects there is need for something else. The search for 'self' can only be met by the story of man, his possibilities, potentialities, achievements, past and present. A selection of literature will answer some questions. Recapitulation of history will answer others. The story of earth evolution, which includes the creator, and the earth's relationship to other heavenly bodies, will add something. A further delving in the sciences will be fruitful but more is needed to show man's development. This can be done by giving a history of art, of poetry, of music, of architecture, of religion. When the bodily instincts awaken, so too, do high ideals and lofty endeavours. Art and its practice and study offer a counter-balance to the pressure of sensual urges.

The scope in literature need be limited only by the capacity of the pupils. Thus their outlook can be widened by the study of travellers' tales, books on exploration, historical novels, biographies and contemporary literature. It is essential for adolescents to use their own faculties of perception and judgement, and specific themes, with indications, should be given them to work out. As an example, they could be asked to contrast the Eumenides of Aeschylus with Shakespeare's Macbeth and to note the change in human experience. In early Greek times the experience of conscience was outside man, personified in the Furies. Man felt himself directed by the gods; today the self-dependant ego-conscious individual has emerged. Conscience is within.

A study of literature includes poetry and drama but the range could be extended to include such matters as the Edda, the Kalevala and the Odyssey. In comparing the works of Dante, Goethe and modern writers, pupils will observe the changing spirit of the times.

With regard to mathematics, adolescents can well exercise their abilities with combinations, permutations, logarithms and trigonometry. Other material would be conic sections, projective geometry and laws of transformation. After the age of fourteen, history and geography should be recapitulated but in a new direction. It is the time to study connections and reasons. Science should now include more chemistry and physics, and also subjects like meteorology and anthropology. Foreign languages should include the study of folk lore, customs and general knowledge of the countries concerned.

On the practical-artistic level there is great scope for activity: woodwork, metalwork, gardening, dress-making or tailoring, cane and basket work, carving, modelling, bookbinding, leatherwork, painting, drawing, singing, drama, choral singing and orchestra where practicable. Where possible it is useful and salutary to give short courses in first aid, surveying, shorthand, typing, and even driving instruction.

There is no denying the fact that some people have an aptitude for intellectual learning and some definitely have not, or that some are gifted in the use of their hands and others are not. It is also a fact that some are not apparently gifted in any way. In the normal run of schools the last mentioned are relegated to the position of nuisances. But gifted with natural talent of one form or another, or not, each child has a claim to education and to as much attention as any other. We have already spoken of eighteen as a suitable leaving-age and also of the necessity to divide the work in certain respects at about the age of sixteen. Besides sharing the general cultural lessons it is of some importance during these years to get away from the four walls of the school in order to gain a wider experience. Therefore visits to farms, factories, mines and concerns of every kind should not be looked upon as extras but as part of the curriculum.

It has become common practice to travel abroad in a school party. Excellent though this may be, it might be even better for pupils to exchange with a school abroad for a term.

This then is an outline of the knowledge and experience which should be given to children and adolescents to accord with their stages of development. It is by no means intended to be exhaustive. The following chart summarises the matter:-

Class 1. Ages 6/7

English: Introduction to writing and reading. Practice in speaking and retelling stories. Recitation of poetry.
Story Material: Fairy stories. Russian folk tales. Grimm.
Mathematics: Introduction to numbers and the four rules.
Modern Foreign Languages: Orally.
Science: Not as such but enlarge knowledge of surroundings in story form.
Music: Singing, recorders, musical appreciation.

Art: Painting, drawing, modelling, from teacher's indica-
tions.
Religion: Not as such but in story form.
Gymnastics: No formal gym but play and games.

Class 2. Ages 7/8

English: Writing, reading, speaking, recitation.
Story Material: Fables and legends.
Mathematics: Mental arithmetic, multiplication tables,
practical problems. Free drawing of shapes as an
introduction to geometry.
Foreign languages: Orally.
Science: Not as such but descriptions of environment,
including flora and fauna.
Music: Singing, recorders, musical appreciation.
Art: Painting, drawing, modelling, from teacher's indica-
tions.
Handwork: Knitting articles.
Religion: Special stories.
Gymnastics: No formal gym. Play and games.

Class 3. Ages 8/9

English: Writing descriptions or retelling stories. Reading,
speaking, recitation. In grammar: parts of speech,
parts of sentence, punctuation.
Story Material: Old Testament stories.
Mathematics: Weights, measures, all possible examples
with four rules. In geometry: shapes, free play with
instruments.
Foreign Languages: Orally.
Science: Not as such but special periods might be given

under the headings of (1) farming and gardening; (2) housebuilding; (3) any other practical activity.

Music: Singing, recorders, appreciation. Staff notation.

Art: Painting, drawing, modelling with more form.

Handwork: Useful articles in any known media.

Religion: Stories. Biographies (Saints). Phenomena of nature.

Gymnastics: Formal exercises accompanied by music or recitation.

Class 4. Ages 9/10

English: Business letters. In grammar; tense, punctuation etc.

Story Material: Norse stories.

Mathematics: Fractions. In geometry: learn names of figures.

Foreign Languages: Reading, writing, grammar.

Science: Special period 'Man and Animal'.

Music: Reading music. Scales. Individual instruments.

Art: Copying now feasible, but not excluding own creative fantasy.

Handwork: Exact sewing, embroidery.

Religion: Stories, biographies.

Gymnastics: With apparatus.

History:)
Geography:)   Study of immediate environment.

Class 5. Ages 10/11

English: Direct and indirect speech. Reporting. Grammar.

Story Material: Greek Stories. Stories from history.

Mathematics: Fractions. Decimals.

Foreign Languages: Grammar, reading, speaking, retelling
   stories. As little translation as possible.
Science: Special study on 'Plants'.
Music: The different keys. Two- and three-part songs.
Art: In connection with other subjects.
Handwork: Making socks and gloves. Stuffed animals.
Religion: Stories. Biographies. The life of Christ.
Gymnastics: With and without apparatus.
History: Ancient civilisations (mythology). India, Persia,
   Egypt.
Geography: Study of the structure, relief and economics of
   the locality, county or country.
Latin:)   If possible.
Greek:)

_____

Class 6. Ages 11/12

English: All forms.
Story Material: Folk lore and background literature for
   other lessons.
Mathematics: Interest, percentage, discount. Practical
   problems. In geometry: theorems.
Foreign Languages: All aspects.
Science: In physics: heat, light, sound, magnetism, electric-
   ity.
Music: Minor scales.
Art: In drawing: projections and shadow drawing.
Handwork: Slippers, skirts.
Religion: Biographies. Life of Christ.
Gymnastics: All forms.
History: Greece and Rome to the Renaissance.
Geography: Of all parts of the earth, leading to geology.
Latin:)   If possible.
Greek:)
Woodwork: Carving simple and practical objects.
Gardening: Practical work.

Class 7. Ages 12 13

English: All aspects.
Story Material: Tales of chivalry. King Arthur.
Mathematics: Squaring, cubing etc. Equations. In geo-
metry: to Pythagoras.
Foreign Languages: All aspects. Literature.
Science: Nutrition and hygiene. Mechanics. In chemistry:
first concepts, chemistry in industry.
Music: Part songs. Contrasting composers. Appreciation.
Art: In drawing: perspective.
Handwork: Shirts, blouses. How materials are made.
Qualities.
Religion: New Testament.
Gymnastics: All forms.
History: Renaissance to 17th Century.
Geography: World economy. Earth and Universe.
Latin:)
Greek:)   If possible.
Woodwork: Moveable toys. Practical articles.
Gardening: Practical work.

Class 8. Ages 13 14

English: All aspects, including epic and dramatic poetry,
business correspondence.
Story Material: Dickens, explorers' tales, anything rele-
vant to main lesson teaching.
Mathematics: Continuation of all aspects. Solid geometry.
Foreign Languages: Literature, poetry, folklore.
Science: Physics and chemistry. Man as a microcosm.
Music: Continued.
Art: Painting from mood of colour.
Handwork: Practical machine-sewn objects.
Religion: New Testament. Biographies. Philosophical ideas.

Gymnastics: All forms.
History: 17th Century to present.
Geography: Economic conditions and culture.
Latin:)
Greek:)   If possible.
Woodwork: Woodcarving.
Gardening: Practical work.

In the next four years (15 to 18) studies are on as wide a scale as possible. Of special value will be the story of the evolution of man as shown through his artefacts of all kinds. Thus special studies could be made in sequence over the next four years of the histories of art, poetry, music, and architecture.

Otherwise the work already started is extended on all sides, to world literature and geography, and to world history, looking at causes. In the sciences one would delve further into botany, chemistry and physics, and also study machines and industrial processes.

Other studies would be anthropology and ethnography There should also be all kinds of handwork, craftwork and art. Continued subjects are music (mixed choir, orchestra, literature and musical appreciation) and foreign languages (all aspects, literature and way of life). On the practical side, subjects would include gardening, practical and theoretical; shorthand; first aid; surveying.

World religions might be given as a final cultural study.

6

The 'How' of Various Subjects

There are various ways of teaching. One can instruct by means of fear — but the idea of standing in front of a class with a stick and drumming the facts in, is dead. One can call upon egotistic ambition; this is still with us in the anti-social form of competition.

A third way is to awaken interest. Modern educational practice says, 'Let the children find out for themselves'. It is true that one learns more by doing than by just looking and listening. It is also true that interest awakens the child's will. To arouse interest all sorts of gimmicks and systems are devised, many of them artificial and unnecessary. The interest will arise through the subject itself if it and the manner of its presentation are related to the child's need and capacity as manifested at the different chronological ages.

We must also bear in mind that the young child has no true power of direction of his own, and in consequence acts arbitrarily. It is a desire of his nature to be told or shown what to do. At the same time the inner moral nature must be cultivated and this can be done through stories. When the good wins and the bad is punished, he is satisfied. This is the beginning of moral development.

Yes, indeed, there are various way of teaching. But there is basically only one way of educating and this lies in a sympathetic understanding of the child. It would be preferable to write 'understanding and love', but the word 'love' has acquired a strange flavour in recent years. The word is appropriate enough if understood in its proper sense.

Much in the general sense of the 'how' in teaching is self-evident. There is the basic human relationship. The child must feel welcome, cared for and valued. Children want to be noticed and have someone take an interest in them. They like to hear their name called so long as it is not a matter of reproof. They need guidance and encouragement. Accomplishment breeds confidence. As already remarked above in the chapter 'Purpose of Education' to educate means to 'nourish'. It is the soul which needs nourishment. Knowledge and experience, served in the right way at the right time, are food and drink. As a child outgrows any given pair of shoes, so does his mind expand and develop. It is essential, therefore, to give ideas which are flexible, and not mere fixed definitions. If the child has to memorise concepts and conclusions, something in him dries up, but living descriptions awaken enthusiasm and joy. Laws do not produce morality: only interest and love do that.

A good teacher will know how to shape his lesson to appeal to all elements in his class. There will be the noisy, rowdy members to whom some dramatic action will have appeal. There will be a few melancholics who may want to sorrow over some sad happening. There will be a collection of dreamers who need to be awakened, as well as the will-o-the-wisps who need a succession of quickly happening events to arrest their attention. Thus, in turn and in some way, all types must be catered for. This presupposes that the teacher has made some study of his pupils and has arrived at some conclusion with regard to their temperament. A knowledge of the temperament of each individual child and the way to treat it educationally is a tremendous asset to a teacher. It is perhaps one of the most important contributions to the 'how' of teaching a child, as distinct from how to teach the subject. In general the emphasis of textbooks is on how to teach the subject and the human element is overlooked. The human element, however, is paramount.

Like an actor, the teacher needs a sense of timing, of climax and anticlimax. For real experience the mood of the class needs to swing. There should be sadness and laughter as well as much that is neutral. Furthermore, in our scientific-objective world, let the teacher not put a brake on his own enthusiasm. If he can teach Pythagoras with spirit or get excited over the difference between a verbal noun and a gerund, then something of this will surely flow over to the pupils.

There can be no set rules in education. It arises out of the living interplay between teacher and taught. The educator's most reliable guide is the chronological development of the human being as set forth above in Chapter Three. The child is developing in time and meeting the static world of space. His experience is different at different ages and the presentation of material must vary in accordance with the change. It is essential to grasp this, if one wishes to understand the child and his needs.

The baby gets cross with the table that 'hit' him. The older child may still get cross but he knows that running into the table was his own fault. Later he will have the sense to avoid the table.

This book is not intended to be a textbook describing how to teach every subject to every age group. In this chapter the attempt will simply be made to show in broad outline how to meet the chronological ages of childhood with a suitable basic approach.

There is, of course, no one way, but thousands. The inventive teacher will always find a new one. Every class, every child and every teacher is different, so there can be no question of a stereotyped method. It is not really a method, in fact, which is being described here but an interpretation of child nature in terms of practical education.

The young child is imitative, and this suggests the obvious way to teach him. Whether we want to teach elementary skills and social behaviour, or to encourage self-development, the path lies through example. Up to the age of six there can be little or no question of formal teaching. The child must have worthy people around him who will talk clearly and sensibly, act sensibly, think sensibly. The child will then be in the right environment.

Reference was made in the previous chapter to the endless things that the child in the nursery can be doing and learning. The secret is to set the example, but whatever is done must not be forced. The person in charge acts and the child instinctively imitates.

As the young child still sees a living quality in things that to the adult are inanimate objects, the nature stories must be such that the objects — be they sun, moon, stars, trees or flowers — can hold converse with one another. The animals can also talk. Myths and fairy tales belong to the early days of humanity and they also belong to the early years of childhood.

Toys which are disguised as teaching material are a fraud. The best playthings are primitive. A rag doll is better than a perfect one because the child's imagination can turn it into a king, princess, beggar or thief according to taste. Irregular blocks rather than cubistic ones are better so that all sorts of shapes can finally emerge. Mechanical toys, where the thinking is built into the apparatus, are stultifying. In support of the last statement one can observe time and time again that a child has no interest in a mechanical toy and only wants to push it.

A few pieces of cloth are sufficient for the actor's wardrobe and dressing-up and acting are excellent occupations. The improvised acting of stories provides scope in many directions, particularly for the development of the imagination.

It is a matter of regret that school life is so often divorced from real life. Where do children get the opportunity of observing practical occupations like ploughing, carpentry, weaving? These used to provide a healthy reality for which we have substituted the 'telly'. For myself, I remember the thrill of standing at the blacksmith's door, watching the fire flare up and the sparks fly as the metal was hammered into shape. Regrettably, this is something which has almost disappeared even from country districts.

Small children do not live in the abstract. There is not much point in trying to describe to them an oak or a chestnut tree, but getting out and finding acorns and conkers is a real experience.

As already noted in the chapter 'Nature of the Child', from the age of seven to fourteen the child experiences the world through his sympathies and antipathies and makes pictures in the mind. Appeal, therefore, must be made during this period to the imagination and the feeling life. Children do not naturally respond to admonition and prohibition, or to reason. Pictorial imagery is effective. The child's mind reacts to descriptions, not explanations or definitions, which only come later. This calls for a basically artistic approach to all subjects and the teacher himself must become an artist.

The Englishman, brought up in the tradition of not showing feeling, and of keeping a stiff upper lip, naturally bristles at the thought of appealing to the feelings, and any mention to him of art or an artistic approach may savour of namby-pamby. It is a prejudice that we have to overcome, at least as far as the education of our children is concerned. It is essential and natural that between seven and fourteen understanding should come about via the feelings. Artistic approach is not to be equated with sentiment, mere painting, or some vague beautifying process.

This type of teaching presupposes that the teacher is able to cultivate an imaginative faculty within himself. He cannot rely on a textbook. Thus, if he is dealing with the animal world, the stress will not be on anatomical, physiological, scientific descriptions but on characterisations. The horse will be a dancing, prancing, light-footed, keenly sensitive friend of man, whose element is really the wind-swept open prairie, and who has served man in manifold ways through thousands of years. One could wax enthusiastic over the shining skin and the rippling muscles underneath. By contrast, the cow is a slow-plodding, near-perfect wandering digestive system, to which fleetness of foot, wariness of eye and intelligence of brain have been sacrificed.

The artist-teacher must also have the faculty of transforming his material into stories which he can present with the necessary drama or otherwise. For instance, instead of describing how the 'four elements' work in plant growth, he can delight the younger children by putting it in this way:

"Once upon a time there was a big brown seed, with white edges and white stripes, which was lying on the ground. The gnomes who lived in that part of the garden knew that it was a seed and that they ought to look after it, so they quietly buried it. Then they told the water fairies about it and the water fairies came down in the rain to give it something to drink. Soon the fire fairies who live in the sun's warmth came on a visit and the seed began to feel strange, as if some change were taking place. It seemed to be getting bigger and soon its jacket burst. One shoot went downwards into the earth and another shoot came up out of the ground. The little shoot that went downwards grew into a root and all the springtime the gnomes were busy looking after it and the soil around it. The rain and the fire fairies kept visiting the growing plant, and the air fairies also came and danced around it. For months it grew, taller than you, and as tall as I am, and then, at the top of the stalk something quite wonderful happened. A huge yellow flower appeared turning its face towards the sun. Some children came to look at it and they said, 'What a big shining face, just like the sun. We will call it a sunflower.' "

When children have crossed the Rubicon of the fourteenth year, the teacher can appeal to their reasoning and understanding faculty.

Let us take a look at the teaching of a particular subject over the years and study the 'how' of teaching English. English in this respect means all aspects of the language — reading, writing, grammar, literature.

The Newsom Report states: 'A wide and generous course of English should do much to prepare the pupils for life in adult society: it is vocational in the best sense'.

A prerequisite of learning is a love of learning, and a prerequisite of learning English is a love of language. We have already said that between the ages of seven and fourteen we must appeal to the imagination, to the feelings, to the sympathies. That is to say, we must make an artistic approach. This is the 'how'.

The first thing to note is that we are dealing with a language, and a language is something that is essentially spoken. People spoke long before writing or reading was invented. It is only a matter of a hundred years since the majority of people in this country have been able to read and write, but they have been able to speak since time immemorial. The child can speak and understand the spoken word long before he can read or write. It is a wonderful process by which the child learns to speak. It is not through concepts but by direct experience of objects and imitation. Think, too, of the small child's delight in making sounds and practising words. The child will learn appreciation of the spoken language by hearing and repeating. Let the teacher, therefore, speak clearly and correctly, but let him do more than this. Let him bring the sounds he makes to consciousness. Let him realise that a vowel expresses something different from a consonant; that the essential character of B is diametrically opposed to that of L. In short, let the teacher cultivate his own speech and the child will instinctively follow his lead.

Interest in and love for sound will be fostered by hearing and speaking poetry. Poetry is sometimes pooh-poohed as something of not much consequence. It has suffered, like singing, in the utilitarian culture of our age. By poetry is meant, not rhymes put together for children, but real poetry. Hear the rolling cadences in Swinburne:

> 'The sea is awake and the sound of the song of her waking is rolled . . .'

See the light, fantastic tripping of the fairy in Shakespeare:

> 'Over hill, over dale,
> Thorough bush, thorough briar,
> Over park, over pale,
> Thorough flood, thorough fire . . .'

Or experience the wonderful sequence of sounds in Fiona MacLeod:

> 'By dim moon glimmering coasts and dim grey wastes
> Of thistle gathered shingle and sea murmuring woods.'

Whether the sense be understood is no great matter at the moment. The sounds themselves, the melody, the rhythm are the pearls of great price. These are the things which the child of six and seven can appreciate, having as yet no understanding for the purely logical and intellectual in language. If it is possible to introduce eurythmy, an art of movement created by Rudolf Steiner, into the curriculum, it will help.

The young child becomes interested in reading or writing because he sees other people doing these things. His own nature is to run and scribble and this provides the clue to a rational way of introducing writing. First of all the mechanics of writing can be practised. Writing consists of lines and loops and curves and circles. A feeling for form can be engendered by letting children run straight lines, curves, loops and circles, which are then afterwards drawn on paper.

In this way the child develops a feeling for form with his whole organism.

Side by side with this, the letter — let us say a consonant in its script form — can be introduced, not as an abstract symbol but from some sort of a picture, actual or imaginative. If we think of 'r' and a series of words beginning with 'r' — race, roll, run, rattle, ram, rat, rip — we find a certain hefty movement expressed. Now let us roll the 'r' in our mouths and draw the movement:

It needs no great stretch of imagination (and children are kindly cooperative in this matter) to derive from this the symbol 'r'.

Another example would be to derive the 'w' from wave.

It is somewhat different with vowels. These are expressions of the inner life, and are far easier to introduce in a phonetic language like German than in English with its hopelessly chaotic spelling of vowel (and other) sounds. It can be done with a little fantasy and an explanation that languages undergo changes from time to time. Thus 'A' (Ah) expresses wonderment in some way; 'O' is a desire to enfold.

In Chapter 3 was mentioned the minor staging post of nine, when the child learns to differentiate between himself and the world, and begins to take a greater interest in outer matters. This is the proper moment to introduce grammar. The child is saying, 'I am here. I am I. Beyond me is something different and separate from me. That is an animal, a tree, a house'. The feeling for the noun arises instinctively. However the artistic story form is still the approach which will most appeal, not the old parrot-like way of learning definitions ('A noun is the name of a person, place or thing'). Something like this would be more appropriate:

> 'When Adam stood in the Garden of Eden, God brought every beast of the field and fowl of the air to him to see what he would call them: and whatsoever Adam called every living creature, that was the name thereof. And Adam gave names to all cattle and to the fowl of the air, and to every beast of the field. Adam saw something flying through the air and he said, "bird". A big animal came lumbering over the fields and he said, "cow". Then he saw a little creature crawling on the ground and he said "snail". To everything which Adam saw he gave a name. Now we can look around us and see all sorts of things and touch all sorts of things. Everything has its name. Noun really means a name'.

There will follow an exciting naming period.

The verb expresses an activity and needs little explanation. It can easily be demonstrated, sometimes boisterously so. Occasionally the teacher can be caught out. I remember once describing the verb enthusiastically in all its activity, with examples like run, skip, hop, jump. Then turning to the class I asked for examples. One melancholic little girl answered, 'I am sitting still'.

A great interest can be awakened for the adjective, the describing word. Ask the children how they would describe some object. Then write or read passages composed mainly of nouns, then with lots of verbs, then adjectives. In this way one soon gets a feeling for the quality of the different parts of speech.

Punctuation can be taught in a similar way, i.e. by experience rather than definition. One can read a story and indicate, by tone or pause, the punctuation. One takes, for instance, a slight breath for a comma, and drops one's voice for the full stop. The idea can be extended to action. The children can stand up for a capital letter, take a breath for a comma, sit down for a full stop, pull the mouth sideways for quotation marks. Indications can be given by gestures.

Clauses and subordinate clauses can also be demonstrated orally in the way of speaking, in the tone or rise and fall of the voice, also pictorially:

'The boy, who had worked hard, was praised'.

In speaking, the relative clause is spoken more quickly.

Pictorially:

'The boy, who had worked hard and done well, was praised'.

Pictorially:

In the matter of handwriting, the practice of freehand form drawing and completing the symmetry of a pattern will further the sense of artistic appreciation and react favourably on the script, e.g. complete the other side:

Or the matter can be done a little more artistically by drawing a reflection picture, e.g. a lake:

(Draw reflection here).

It should not be thought that this approach obviates work and routine practice. Good handwriting and spelling can be looked upon as social necessities. Reading, writing and speaking need continual practice in accordance with the capacity. The reading material obviously progresses in difficulty and the matter is scaled to the child's age and comprehension.

To accord with the child's mental development, written work should consist of simple compositions, the retelling of stories or incidents, descriptions and letters. Before the age of twelve it is too early to expect work containing original logical sequences. The modern craze for comprehension exercises at an early age dulls the imagination.

The usefulness of drama should not be overlooked, but this is now widely recognised, and calls for no further elaboration.

Oral work is good at any age. This means talking to the children and letting them talk as well. There must be order. If one child is talking the rest must learn to listen. Talking to children is frowned upon in some circles. Another personal experience will explain best what is meant here. For years I had been in the habit of talking to classes of children, explaining, describing, questioning, getting their contributions, and a pleasant friendly atmosphere resulted. One day an inspector came in. He was impressed with the atmosphere and 'the pleasant fatherly attitude'. But he went on to admonish me for not putting into practice the latest idea that children must find out things for themselves. As some of these children, aged eleven and twelve, could scarcely read or write, there was a certain difficulty (I was teaching geography and their lack of skills was not my fault). However, willing to bring myself up-to-date and comply, I embarked on a new method by handing out books and questionnaires and restricted myself to helping the children to help themselves. The result was nervousness, irritability and a general restlessness. After a few weeks a pathetic little group came to me with the question, 'Why don't you talk to us any more?'

At twelve to thirteen an independent aesthetic appreciation begins to dawn. Therefore, this is the time to begin to study the artistic forms of language as such, i.e. prose and poetry. In poetry the different forms can be studied, such as epic, lyric, dramatic. Again the manner of presentation is via the thing itself, developing a feeling or appreciation for whatever is involved, followed by explanations. A general appreciation of literature and language will have been fostered throughout the years by means of reading, both class and individual reading, and by the teacher reading and letting the children listen without following the text in their own books.

At fourteen the inner world awakens and also a tremendous interest in the world around. The adolescent seeks rational explanations. The paramount questions are 'How?' and 'Why?'. So how does one teach pupils from the age of fourteen onwards? One answers the questions which arise consciously or subconsciously. Or, since adolescents are capable of independent work, one directs their attention to where answers may be found. Such questions refer to general matters such as the world order, destiny, evolution, man's nature, religious beliefs. Specifically in English lessons one can explain the basis of grammar, which is not something superimposed on language but something which has grown out of human experience. The verb is connected with willing, the noun with thinking, and the adjective with feeling.

In the next year one can go further into the history and development of the mother tongue, its peculiarities and the uses of figures of speech. Rational explanations are required. Why, for instance, do we use metaphors and similes? We must refer to human evolution. Like the child between seven and fourteen the mind needs a picture to help comprehension. 'He jumped quickly' says very little. 'He jumped like greased lightning' says much more. In derivations we often find hidden metaphors. It is a process of the mind that what was once a picture becomes a concept. We know very well what a derivation is but at the moment of using the word we do not usually recall the ancestry. (Latin *de*, meaning 'from', and *rivus*, 'river'.) Similarly, as concepts we know what 'capricious' and 'capering' mean, but do we know that they are derived from *caper*, a goat?

If pupils are still at school after sixteen, the emphasis should be on literature, but essay writing, précis and other routine work can always be practised to achieve a higher standard of perfection. A few lessons on official jargon and form-filling might also be useful.

In mathematics as in all other subjects, the essential thing is to consider the nature of the child. This is not necessarily to be equated with capability or desire. A child may be capable or desirous of doing all sorts of things which are not good for him at that particular moment. We are hoping to develop a balanced, well integrated personality and must always bear in mind organic development.

The obvious thing here again is to appeal to the rhythmic-artistic-imaginative forces. The child of six or seven is still starry-eyed and the first arithmetic lessons should be in a story form. A former pupil of mine recently remarked with what joy she had first learned the rudiments of mathematics thirty years ago through a story which had been told to the class. Roughly it was as follows:

'A princess was being wooed by several princes. She lived in a high tower and leading up to it was a flight of steps. The first prince came up like this: 1,2,3, etc. But he took a long time and the princess refused him. The next came 2,4,6, etc. The next came up in threes and so it went on. (Thus we built up the tables). One day, a prince came, took one look at the princess, and with one leap landed in her arms. 'My hero!' said the princess, and they got married and lived happily ever after'.

Number work is helped by rhythmic movement, be it running, clapping or jumping. In a way similar to the above story one counts 1,2,3; 4,5,6; 7,8,9; etc., stamping or clapping on the third number or whatever it is. As mentioned in the last chapter, numbers are not only units for counting but have a qualitative value and children will be interested to learn something about one-ness, two-ness, and so on. As a simple illustration one could talk about the head as a unity but the hands as a duality and children immediately appreciate the difference.

As already noted, in the early years the child still sees the world as a unity and this persists to the age of nine or ten. The organic way of teaching arithmetic is then to go from the whole to the parts. One sees a wood before the individual trees. One sees a crowd before individuals in it. Thus the teacher can take an apple, cut it through, and show how the two pieces make the whole again. Then he divides it into quarters, or he can have counters, representing, say, a herd of twelve cows. Now the children explore the various possibilities of twelve: six in one stall, six in another; three in four stalls; or four in three. Twelve cows are in a field but two get through the hedge. How many are left? Another time the farmer comes to look for his twelve cows but finds only nine. How many have escaped? And so on. Out of a living concept the children experience the four rules.

Since we are also concerned with moral education, we should perhaps ponder on the difference in starting from the whole and proceeding to the parts, and the reverse. To add is to collect to oneself. To subtract or divide from a whole and share out has the quality of generosity.

Children love rhythmic chanting and there is no reason why they should not master their tables in this way even if they do not fully understand them. It is a fallacy to think that only what is immediately understood should be taught. It is not the way of a child. Children — and grown-ups — learn many things which they only understand later.

The age of nine is the time for practical tasks and in mathematics this means all sorts of practical problems in weights and measures. Still, the story form is the best approach, and fortunately the historical development of weights and measures is fascinating. Why did people want to measure? How did they fix a standard? The children will find the story of the furlong (furrow long) and the rod, pole or perch (the drover's stick) and all the rest of these oddities very interesting. Even if they are disappearing the stories about them are still worth telling, as they connect weights and measures with reality.

When the unified view of the world begins to break up into subjects at about the age of ten, that is the time for fractions. The introduction to these can be on similar lines to the first introduction to arithmetic, but it is also necessary to explain how one sometimes has to deal with bits and pieces. The work should be kept within the realm of likelihood.

With the child's greater awareness of the physical world at twelve, the appropriate mathematical work should be even more in connection with the problems of practical life and, one might add, *practical* problems! I once noticed a teacher setting problems of this order: find 79.55% of £126.77. As a mental exercise this may be excellent but it seems a little remote from practical reality. The work therefore should be everyday problems in interest, discount, exchange etc., with explanations of the use of cheques and the banking system.

A step can now be made into the more theoretical realm of algebra   with   formulae   as   a   starting   point,   e.g.

l × b = length × breadth; area of a triangle = ½ (base × height).

In geometry, the younger children will get interested and involved if they are allowed and encouraged to draw patterns in which they themselves perceive certain developments or laws. For the moment there need be no question of formulating these.

At nine or ten, of his own volition, the child will wish to use instruments and take pride in exactness. As with weights and measures, his interest will be kindled by learning what geometry is about and by hearing of its origins.

The third stage, belonging to the ages of twelve and onward is a matter of cognition. Work has been done, now one looks at it, forms conclusions, passes judgement and arrives at the concept. The child will have learnt many things practically, or have experienced them visually, as for example, the theorem of Pythagoras; now is the time for formal proof. With the expanding consciousness and the reasoning faculty at fourteen all mathematical work in its conceptual form is in place.

The whole field of history is far too vast to handle in school, yet it should be attempted. History is the story of man's development. Its purpose is to give the human being some information about himself in the time sequence. Each human being is a part of history and his contribution to the world makes future history. To deal only with a certain period, as is so often done, is to give a stunted, crippled outlook. Therefore one has to attempt to take the whole in some measure.

History begins in mythology and legend and leads to the present. The ancient peoples had not such a clear thinking consciousness as modern man, nor has the child. Therefore the two — the ancient peoples and the child — go hand in hand. Only at the age of twelve is the child really ready to understand history proper. History can and should be taught earlier, but the early teaching will have to consist of pictures and descriptions. Thus the mythologies are the proper material at first, followed by single scenes from the past, stories or biographies. At twelve things begin to fit into a pattern and the more pieces one has of a pattern the broader the final picture.

History is often taught as something separate from man. That is probably one of the reasons why it has little appeal to some children. History is not a string of dates and battles, but a story of cultural development. The child first has to realise a time element and that he himself is a part of this element and a part of history. This can be fostered by speaking of events which took place in his father's day, his grandfather's and his great-grandfather's. If the teacher can say, 'My father used to tell me', or 'Your father used to do so and so', he has a great asset. In this way a feeling of continuity and belonging is created. In actual fact a surprisingly small number of generations takes us back to William the Conqueror or even the birth of Christ. *Our* ancestors experienced these events and so a personal relationship with historical figures and happenings is established.

To study a single period as a series of isolated and independent events is nonsense. The achievements of the Greeks and Romans, for instance, are intimately connected with the present and the idea of continuity must be conveyed. The present is the result of the past and the future will be the result of the present. There are no divisions. Causes and effects, happenings and results, are things which will be understood more and more during the adolescent years.

As with most teaching and contrary to much that is advocated in modern education, the vital factor is the teacher, not the textbook. The latter may be useful for reference but in teaching history the teacher has to be able to digest the facts and reproduce in his descriptions the personalities of history and events so that they live in his recreation before the mind's eye of the pupil.

Since one cannot encompass the whole course of history, it

is necessary to teach 'symptomatically'. That is to say, one presents certain typical events or personalities which will illustrate a whole period. A case in point could be Leonardo da Vinci. Here is a combination of artist, scientist, sculptor and engineer. He is known as the father of perspective; he built bridges and tunnels, and designed an aeroplane, besides all the work by which he is better known. One could say that Leonardo was a symptom of the new technological age which was about to break in upon the world. Similarly, the teachings and lives of Luther, Wycliffe, Huss, are symptoms of man's striving towards independence and freedom.

The 'how' of teaching geography follows the same pattern of expanding consciousness — neighbourhood, then further afield, world, cosmos. Bearing in mind that the logical faculty is not truly awake until fourteen, the presentation of geography up to that age is in pictures and descriptions. To foster a feeling of responsibility, emphasis could be laid on the fact that the earth gives so much. Gradually the question will arise as to what man does with these gifts, and one thus arrives at economic geography. This would be proper about the ages of thirteen and fourteen. Following this, given the development of the child's sense of individuality, it is natural to connect culture with geography. This is the correct time, too, for mathematical geography. Eventually one connects up with the geology and astronomy.

There is endless scope for map work, sketches, diagrams, even painting and modelling.

Only after fourteen is it possible to aim at comprehensive understanding of geography, and to link things properly together, such as natural resources, industries, economics, culture, peoples, international law.

In the matter of learning foreign languages, child nature again points the way. The mother tongue is learned through imitation. Although this faculty is waning at six when the child should start school, it is still evident to some degree.

Therefore the first lessons in the foreign tongue should be given at this age, by way of listening and repeating. This can be done in many ways — learning poems, phrases, songs, commands, conversation pieces, plays. A child who is exposed to several languages in his early years learns them all. One might think that he would get them mixed up, but by some curious gift, this is not the case.

If nine is the right age for grammar of the mother tongue, it is also the right age for the grammar of foreign languages, although, as a matter of convenience, it could follow.

As with the learning of multiplication tables, in foreign languages children enjoy rhythmic chanting. There can be no objection to their learning verbs and declensions by rote even if these are not fully understood. To have them stored away in the memory is useful, and in due course they are able to draw upon them and understand them.

As far as possible, direct experience is best. This encourages thinking in the foreign tongue and translation should be kept to a minimum, at least for the younger children. Later and for professional purposes, translation is a good exercise.

As a foreign language belongs to a particular people inhabiting a particular part of the earth, there should be some coordination with the geography teaching. Thus, about the age of fourteen, foreign folk tales and customs should find a place in the syllabus.

From fourteen onwards the capacity to learn naturally increases, and the work in grammar, vocabulary, writing and reading can be intensified. Where time allows, the origin, construction and literature of the language may well be carefully and thoughtfully studied.

Since natural science deals with the earth in its physical material sense, the obvious age for beginning to teach science proper is twelve. Nevertheless a great deal should have been learnt by this time, through various studies already made which are usually classed under the heading of science.

We have already spoken of 'man and animal' and 'plant' periods at the ages of ten and eleven respectively. They were artistic appreciations which will have awakened interest. Having in some way thus connected himself emotionally, the child will be well prepared, after fourteen, to make a more scientific study. As far as man and animals are concerned the subjects now become anatomy and physiology.

With regard to plants, one would have described the qualities, colour and scent of flowers, leaf formation and transformation, the whole process of plant growth, the connections with the elements. At twelve more utilitarian aspects may well have been considered, such as the uses of timber, edible plants, herbs as medicines. Then, from fourteen onwards, detailed study is in place.

In geology, the approach is best made through a study of those rocks, such as chalk and limestone, which have been formed from living creatures. A suitable bridge is thus formed to the inorganic world.

In general the approach to science should be via the phenomena. At the age of twelve the dawning thinking capacity needs practice. The right path is nevertheless from the artistic to the intellectual, from music to acoustics, from colour to optics and light. The phenomena, — for example, in connection with heat and electricity can be shown, and the relevant laws developed from them.

Similarly the fundamentals of mechanics are demonstrated — lever, wheel, axle, pulley, inclined plane — and the laws deduced.

The approach to chemistry is the same and should be made about the same time. No hypothesis should be first stated and then the proof demonstrated. Let the pupils discover the laws themselves. Here the idea of letting children find out for themselves is in its right place. Descriptions of the world are the right material from seven to fourteen; now explanations are needed and if they can be discovered by the pupils themselves, so much the better.

In the upper school all the various studies should be continued as far as possible, but they should also be brought into connection with practical matters, such as engines of all types, chemical processes in industry, architecture, and agriculture.

Now is a suitable time for pupils to do project work. Now is the time for individual effort. The work as a whole at this time should have that character, but in many fields it is impossible for the pupil to cover the ground, as for instance the surveys mentioned in the last chapter on art, music, religion and architecture. It is therefore the role of the teacher at this stage to become the director. He will gather the information he thinks necessary, point out other sources, coordinate and, of course, correct.

The development of the human mind, historically and individually, is from imagination, through pictorial imagery to conceptual thinking and this is the golden thread that the teacher must follow in teaching his pupils.

The teaching of religion is a somewhat neglected subject, but religion has been one of the most potent forces in the world from time immemorial. It is a subject which should be in every school curriculum, but it cannot be handled except by a teacher who does so with conviction. What, then, is a religious lesson and what is its content?

Religion, or religious belief or religious experience is something universal. From the earliest times the human being has felt himself surrounded by powers which he has not understood. He has experienced beings in the plants, in the thunder, in the starry heavens. He has pondered on the alternation of day and night and the change of the seasons. He has puzzled over the origin of the universe, the earth and his own place therein. It is the common striving of man to try to come to terms with the universe, and to understand himself. All religions are founded in this. Kant's famous dictum was a religious experience: 'Two things impress me above all others. One is the starry world without; the other, the moral law within'.

In our scientific-technological age we have measured the distances to the stars, we have even put men on the moon, we have analysed the human mind. Knowing so much and understanding so much (on one level) we no longer develop awe and reverence towards the creation. We either ignore it or attempt to explain it scientifically. Yet deep within ourselves there is the inescapable feeling of mystery and of the presence of some supersensible element. It has a thousand names. Call it God, the master mind, the spiritual world, what you will.

The religion lesson is, therefore, something very special. Its task is to assure the soul of its connection with the divine. This is something that need not be based on the Bible, even in a Christian country, although the Bible is a good source of teaching material. In a Christian country it is natural to teach Christianity, but it would be wrong to try to guide pupils into any particular form or to instil particular beliefs which we ourselves may hold.

What, then, shall we teach? How? The answer to 'What?' is almost anything — there are 'sermons in stones, books in the running brooks and good in everything'. The presentation, however, must arouse a deeper experience. Such feelings as wonder, appreciation, reverence, awe, patience, humility, gratitude, devotion are all akin to religious feeling. A mere injunction to respect or admire something, or be grateful for it, is no use at all. The effect must be indirect. What is given must touch the right chord without any moral sermon.

As with everything else, moreover, the content and the way of presentation of religion must be related to the child's age. Up to the age of nine the child feels at one with his surroundings. Inanimate as well as animate objects can hold converse with one another. The fairies or the gnomes or the animals will help those who are good to them. Children derive great satisfaction from stories where the good triumphs, and this in itself builds a sense for what is right and wrong.

Stories, therefore, with this theme, are in place at this age, but also stories containing some element of the miraculous are good nourishment. Such will be found in the legends of the saints, such as Francis, Martin, Nicholas, Christopher, Patrick, Columba, Hilda and Michael, to mention but a few. At Christmas the Christ legends of Selma Lagerlöf are particularly suitable.

Besides stories as such, anything is useful which characterises the things of earth and human power as gifts of God. There is much to arouse a religious feeling in the phenomena of nature. Think, for instance, of a grain of corn or a drop of water or the arrival of a new baby and consider the wonder of these things.

At the age of nine or ten there comes a certain separation of the self from the rest of the world. The child is more conscious of other people, and this entails greater consciousness of self. Stories, therefore, either fictitious or real, can be given which deal with personal destiny. Some of the stories of the saints are useful here, as also biographies showing personal struggles and the overcoming of what might be termed a bad destiny. The latter category includes the lives of, for example, Helen Keller or Lord Nelson (as a child weak and sickly); the former category covers such characters as Grenfell of Labrador, Shaftesbury, Booker Washington. By the same token, this is the time to introduce stories from the life of Christ (Selected Old Testament stories also have a place and contain ethical instruction, as already referred to).

With the child's thinking capacity developing at thirteen and fourteen, one can proceed to a more thorough study of one of the Gospels. It accords with the child's mind to learn of the sacrifice and victory of Christ. Then the other Gospels can be studied, as the pupils will now appreciate that events can be seen from more sides than one. The adolescent begins to be assailed by doubts, to be more conscious of the existence of evil. He needs reassurance of the existence of good and the ultimate triumph of the human spirit. This, again, can be illustrated from the biographies of such people as Nansen, William Booth, Gladys Aylward. The lives of St. Paul and St. Augustine also provide good material and, of course, the Acts of the Apostles. Further themes can be taken from the Arthurian legends of the Holy Grail.

In his gropings for truth the adolescent can be helped by much other material, e.g. descriptions of customs or beliefs of peoples who live much closer to nature than we do; in particular, their attitudes towards the divine, towards death, the dead and the after-life. This must not be done in a cynical we-know-better way but as an attempt to arouse a genuine feeling for the beyond. Such themes would lead to further discussions on matters like reincarnation and personal destiny. Answers can be gained from religious or philosophic sources which will not be dogmatic, final answers, but give food for thought.

Finally, it can be shown that in all religions there are similar qualities and strivings; a history of religions can show the human spirit in its eternal quest for truth. All religions are genuine but we also have to show Christianity as a culmination.

The above is concerned with what can be done in the specifically religious lesson. Throughout other teaching there are many opportunities to foster the qualities enumerated. They can be found in music, art, poetry, language. But in the religion lesson the special emphasis must be in creating a mood, in fostering a feeling for the living spirit in all things.

7

Teachers and Taught

Whatever ideas may be put forward with regard to education, they are of no use without someone to carry them out. The quality of the teacher determines the quality of the education and to a great extent the development of the child. It is an enormous responsibility. There are teachers who are time-servers. There are teachers, known to me personally, whose task — by choice — lies in working with deprived Negro children in one of America's large cities. Some teachers are good technicians in the sense that they have the capacity to train children to pass examinations. Some teachers are capable, responsible people devoted to their pupils, and there are some whose talents would definitely be better applied elsewhere.

For a teacher it is not a question of learning something in order to teach it again, and to teach it in the same way. This is one of the sins of the past, as, for example, when the university graduate was considered capable of teaching without any teacher training. Now at least that has been remedied; but whether university trained or college trained, or both, it is not sufficient for a teacher to have merely acquired a certain knowledge of things and psychological theories, mixed with a little practical work. Teachers should not be examined so much on what they know, as on whether they have the ability, the patience, the persistence, the temperament for establishing a relationship with children.

Teaching is a matter of maturity, not necessarily in age. For the teacher himself the question must be forever in his mind as to whether, in all conscience, he can accept the responsibility of standing before children in the way required of him.

It is also wrong that young people should leave school, enter training college, qualify and return immediately to teach. It means that they have scarcely been out of the four walls. They have the minimum knowledge required for their work and little knowledge of the outside world. They may have drifted into teaching without any sense of vocation. Children should be taught by practical people with some experience of life. To some extent this is now being brought about through the entry into colleges of mature students. It would also be a good thing for teachers to step out of teaching after a few years for a break. A year in farming, or industry, or business would help them to keep their feet on the ground.

In the same line of thought it would be a leaven in the schools if people from other walks of life were invited in to take part from time to time. In some schools the police are regular visitors to talk on road safety or other aspects of their work. This idea could well be extended, and a farmer, a fireman, lawyer, doctor, industrialist might well have a great deal to contribute. Many might even welcome the opportunity. Obviously, if such a specialist were to take part for any length of time, it would be necessary to ensure that he had some teaching ability.

It is beyond the scope of the present work to discuss the whole field of teacher training. Let it be said simply that it appears to be inadequate. To amass the requisite knowledge, to practise the arts, to study the child and to have some in-training requires more than three years.

What is then required of a teacher, or let us say an educator in the best sense? That he has mastered his material and digested it, is a *sine qua non*. But knowing something and being able to teach it are two vastly different things. The teacher needs the knowledge of the material and the knowledge of the nature of the child. Theories about education and methods and systems may be many but in the final analysis teachers are needed who can deal with children. The beginning, middle and end of good teaching is a study of the child. All other knowledge is to be found in books. Some knowledge of the child and child nature is also to be found in books, otherwise this one might not have been written. But the knowledge of the particular children with which one particular teacher deals is only obtained from day-to-day observation and one could even go so far as to say, a nightly meditation; for knowing the child does not mean external observation only. The conscientious teacher never has the child very far from his thoughts, and, as in every other sphere, it is good to reflect on matters and events, so is it good practice for a teacher to think about his children when they are not immediately in front of him. This is possible if the manner of teaching, i.e. the class teacher arrangement, as here advocated, is practised. Where a specialist teacher ranges over all classes and has many children for short periods, the thing is obviously next to impossible, which fact speaks against such an arrangement.

Clearly, good teaching calls for a special breed of teachers, not time-servers, not technicians, but human beings with the necessary knowledge and feeling of responsibility, interested in other human beings. Such teachers must be socially minded enough to get together and consider certain classes which they take and even certain individual children. Experience shows that when teachers simply discuss among themselves a child with some particular difficulty, the child invariably improves, although they may not have found any specific solution. It may be that apart from gaining a better insight into the child through the various points of view, the general attention is focused on the child, who responds. Something like this should become general pedagogical practice.

Children vary from day to day. Being not yet in possession of themselves, or only partially so, they are influenced by all sorts of extraneous matters such as the weather and the environment. A child can also be much influenced by an internal matter such as indigestion or a bruised soul from some reproach.

We have mentioned already that a class will be very differently behaved on a stormy day than on a hot sunny one. The teacher may have come into class with an excellently prepared lesson but, if he is at all susceptible, he may suddenly feel that what he has prepared will not be received as he anticipated. Then he must be flexible and mentally agile enough to switch his approach or even do something else. The inspector will no doubt come in at that moment.

Every book on teaching, every lecturer, every inspector recommends the teacher to keep the child's interest. The practical teacher knows this better than anyone, but he also knows that it is not always possible. There is always some grind. Nevertheless, the advice is correct and the key to keeping most of the child's interest lies in what we have described above. We must keep in tune with child nature. However, the teacher also has to watch that he does not become sour or stereotyped, trotting out his little prejudices and corny jokes year after year. Though in a different sense, he too is still growing and still learning. If he can go on learning his mind will remain agile, and this is a sort of built-in safeguard in the class teacher arrangement. He teaches a variety of subjects for eight years and then starts again. The world has meantime changed, so he never really repeats. He must be forever creative, and that is certainly a very good thing for his charges.

The teacher might also do well to reflect on what effect, even physical effect, his own personality may have on the children. If he is a fiery type, stampeding and bellowing, he may well give them shocks. If he is a bore, maybe their blood will just cease to flow. The teacher's external appearance should be clean and moderately tidy, and his state of soul likewise. He must always strive towards harmony within himself. If he has personal troubles, then let him leave these on the doorstep when he enters the classroom. Let him also keep his mind active in the eternal search for knowledge and let him cultivate his talents. The best teachers will be those who, besides possessing the natural qualities, seek to improve themselves, not in the material sense, not only in their attempts to learn more and teach better, but in their own character. It has been well said that children will learn more from what a teacher is than from what he teaches.

There is one more thing of paramount importance. The teacher must be free. In his essay 'Liberty', John Stuart Mill says that it is not the function of the government to administer education, but to protect the rights of those who do — the parents and teachers. This was written when universal education was just being mooted. It still applies. Education must be free to develop in its own right and not be subject to political or economic pressures. It is concerned with human development, not cogs in a machine.

Finally, what of the pupils? The education here described aims to be comprehensive in every sense. It touches all aspects of life and awakens all human talents. It seeks to give light of knowledge, depth of feeling and strength of will. It is for all children — slow, medium or fast learners. Some pupils may later occupy important positions in life and some be in more lowly stations. Whether they become cabinet ministers or labourers, managers or clerks, is immaterial. These are not the criteria by which education must be judged. The true measure of education is the final quality of the individuals, as human beings, with whom it deals.

Bibliography

Rudolf Steiner gave many lecture cycles, courses and single lectures to many different audiences, in different places and at different times. A certain element of repetition is therefore to be expected. All the lectures are now available in book form and the following is a selection of those on education:

Modern Values in Education
A Modern Art of Education
The Study of Man
Practical Course for Teachers
The Spiritual Ground of Education
The Kingdom of Childhood
The Essentials of Education
The Roots of Education

One written work is:

The Education of the Child in the Light of Anthroposophy

Fundamental works of Rudolf Steiner elucidating the Anthroposophical, or spiritual scientific, world conception are:

The Philosophy of Freedom
Occult Science
Theosophy (To be understood in the original meaning of "Divine Wisdom")
Knowledge of the Higher Worlds. How is it Achieved?

The above are published by Rudolf Steiner Press, London.

A general introduction to the life and work of Rudolf Steiner is:

Rudolf Steiner by Johannes Hemleben (Henry Goulden, Pub.)

The author of Commonsense Schooling has written a series of educational guides, giving practical advice on the teaching of various subjects:

> *The Curriculum of the Rudolf Steiner School*
> *Teaching English*
> *Teaching Mathematics*
> *'Teaching Geography*
> *Practical Activities (Farming, Gardening, Housebuilding)*
> *Man and Animal*
> *Plant Study/Geology*
> *Physical Sciences I (Physics)*
> *Physical Sciences II (Chemistry)*
> *Nutrition, Health, Anthropology*
> *History: The Ancient Civilisations – India, Persia, Egypt, Babylon, Greece, Rome*
> *History: From the Renaissance to the Second World War*

Other Books by Roy Wilkinson:

Rudolf Steiner on Education – a digest of all Rudolf Steiner's work on the subject.

Questions and Answers on Rudolf Steiner Education – the most popular short statement in print.

The Temperaments – a practical guide to their recognition and to ways of using them educationally.

Miscellany – a few original poems and a note on Gymnastics.

Old Testament Stories – Dr. Steiner recommends that children should read the Old Testament stories for themselves after they have heard them. This collection covers all the books of the Old Testament and the author has included certain indications given by Dr. Steiner which lead to clarification of the text.

Commentary on the Old Testament Stories – This work gives an interpretation and an explanation of the stories in the light of Rudolf Steiner's spiritual science. It will be of particular use to teachers in helping them to understand the background of the stories, which, from an educational point of view, should be given to children at the age of nine or ten.

The Interpretation of Fairy Tales – One could base a whole course of spiritual science on the wisdom in Fairy Tales. Here are summaries of some forty of the most popular stories with an explanation of the background.

The Norse Stories and their Significance – Summaries of the most important stories, and explanations.

Roy Wilkinson has also written a series of booklets dealing in outline with various aspects of life from the Anthroposophical point of view. They embrace such questions as World Evolution, the Being of Man, Destiny, the Inner Life etc.

All the titles by Roy Wilkinson are available from The Robinswood Press, Stourbridge, England.